directions

new FOR
HIGHER
EDUCATION

n u m b e r 1 0
summer 1975

new directions for higher education

a quarterly sourcebook edited by
JB Lon Hefferlin

number 10
summer 1975

individualizing education by learning contracts

neal r. berte
issue editor

Jossey-Bass Inc., Publishers
San Francisco · Washington · London

INDIVIDUALIZING EDUCATION BY LEARNING CONTRACTS
New Directions for Higher Education
Volume III, Number 2, Summer 1975
    Neal R. Berte, Issue Editor

Copyright © 1975 by Jossey-Bass, Inc., Publishers
              and
              Jossey-Bass Limited

New Directions for Higher Education is published quarterly
by Jossey-Bass, Inc., Publishers. Subscriptions are available
at the regular rate for institutions, libraries, and agencies
of $25 for one year. Individuals may subscribe at the special
professional rate of $15 for one year. *New Directions* is
numbered sequentially—please order extra copies by sequential
number. The volume and issue numbers above are included for
the convenience of libraries. Second-class postage rates paid
at San Francisco, California, and at additional mailing offices.

Correspondence:
Subscriptions, single-issue orders, change of address notices,
undelivered copies, and other correspondence should be sent to
New Directions Subscriptions, Jossey-Bass, Inc., Publishers,
615 Montgomery Street, San Francisco, California 94111.
Editorial correspondence should be sent to the Editor-in-Chief,
JB Lon Hefferlin, at the same address.

Library of Congress Catalogue Card Number LC 75-13734

Cover design by Willi Baum
Manufactured in the United States of America

contents

editor's notes   *neal r. berte*   vii

Learning contracts defined, and the rationale of this issue explained.

individualization and contracting   *neal r. berte*   1

An analysis of the underlying concepts and unique contributions of learning contracts to higher education.

learning contracts at   *james feeney*   9
new college, sarasota   *gresham riley*

Why and how the first institution to employ learning contracts introduced the idea, from the perspective of three years' experience.

developing intellectual competence   *arthur w. chickering*   31
at empire state

Examples of how Empire State College in New York uses learning contracts together with first results of students' evaluation of their use.

contracting in a university without   *argentine s. craig*   41
walls program

The experience of UWW at Morgan State College in Maryland with contracts, including costs of the program.

out-of-class contract learning at   *john duley*   53
justin morrill

Three uses of contracts at Michigan State's Justin Morrill College—in cross-cultural field study, independent study, and community project field education.

bringing about change in   *neal r. berte*   65
a traditional university

Four students at New College of the University of Alabama illustrate how an innovative unit of an institution can use contracting to experiment with institution-wide changes.

advising for goal development and   *bernard j. sloan*   **77**
assessment of educational resources

> Suggestions for strengthening the advisor or mentor relationship
> of faculty member to student in order to assure the success of
> contracting.

evaluating individualized learning   *harold l. hodgkinson*   **83**

> How individualized programs require individualized assessment
> of student achievement, and how these programs can themselves
> be assessed.

the future for learning contracts   *neal r. berte*   **93**

> A summary of the strengths and weaknesses of contracting, and
> of the factors educators should consider in adopting the idea on
> their campus.

index   **101**

editor's notes

Learning contracts are written agreements or commitments between a student and a faculty member or faculty committee regarding a particular amount of student work and the institutional reward or credit for this work.

Individualizing education for students through learning contracts is a concept which has gained increased prominence in higher education in recent years. Probably most educators would agree that the individualization of learning is a good ideal but that also it is extremely difficult to accomplish. This issue includes both the philosophical rationale and the practical realities of individualization by various approaches to contract learning. The articles provide the particular and detailed information needed by educators who are contemplating the use of learning contracts in their own institutions.

In the first article I develop the concept of contract learning and attempt to set it in perspective within the larger context of higher education. The next five articles offer examples of the diversity involved in the learning contract movement, beginning with the institution that first adopted the approach in 1964—New College at Sarasota, Florida—and examining in turn Empire State College, the University Without Walls program of Morgan State College, Justin Morrill College at Michigan State University, and the New College of the University of Alabama. Following these examples, the final two articles discuss recurring themes important in the movement. Bernard J. Sloan emphasizes the "goal development" process in contract learning—a critical ingredient in this approach to college education. Harold L. Hodgkinson then examines the problem of evaluating individualized programs such as contract learning. And I conclude with a discussion of the present strengths and weaknesses of contract learning programs and a prognosis about their future.

The institutions and authors represented in this issue are chosen because of the diversity of approaches and the leadership they present in the use of the contract learning concept. I am grateful to these authors as well as to others involved in the preparation of the volume: Elaine Hughey Barnes and Eddie O'Neil, two graduates of the New College at the University of Alabama, who provided research assistance for it.

Not all of the illustrations and implications of learning contracts in higher education could be covered in this sourcebook. However, the University of Alabama Press later this summer will publish *A Comprehensive Analysis of Individualization through Contract Learning.* That volume will expand upon the present papers and contain additional material by John Bilorusky and Harry Butler. The reader whose interest in contracting is whetted by the present volume can refer later to that book for more ideas.

It will be obvious to the reader of this volume that learning contracts mean different things to different people. It will be equally obvious that their use is not a panacea for the ills of higher education. But contracting can help American colleges and universities open up a greater variety of educational paths and create a more diverse series of options to meet the needs of their students so that each of them can maximize their opportunities in higher education, based on their own aims and interests.

Neal R. Berte
Issue Editor

How learning contracts relate to the
entire movement toward individually
tailored programs of education.

individualization and contracting

neal r. berte

Over the past decade, the terms *contract* and *contracting* have developed at least three new uses in American higher education: growth contracting, contracting for grades, and learning contracts. All three concepts are related, but each is distinct; only the third is the major subject of this volume.

Growth contracting involves a faculty or staff member agreeing with an administrative superior or colleague at the beginning of a contract term, such as the academic year, about his responsibilities and obligations during this period, emphasizing particular areas of professional growth. At the end of the term, the two discuss progress over the period, thus encouraging self-evaluation and reflection by the faculty or staff member about his aims, interests, and accomplishments.

Contracting for grades involves an agreement between a teacher and a student at the beginning of a course as to the grade the student expects to receive and the amount and quality of work he is expected to produce to earn this grade. In this way, students are aware of what is expected of them right from the start of the course and they can progress without the fear and anxiety associated with ambiguous expectations or evaluations (Dash, 1970).

1

Learning contracts, in contrast, are agreements between a student and teacher over almost everything about a learning experience: its focus, scope, methods, duration, and evaluation—not necessarily an eventual grade. Though not binding in a strictly legal sense, learning contracts are statements of agreement on at least four elements: (1) the student's goals for the particular learning experience, (2) the methods by which the student aims to accomplish these goals, (3) the evaluation measures to be employed in assessing this achievement, and (4) the amount of credit to be awarded the student as a result of the achievement.

underlying concepts of learning contracts

Underlying learning contracts are the concepts that not merely a student's grade but all the arrangements for learning can be mutually negotiated between a student and a teacher, and that this mutual agreement in advance of learning is desirable for the learning process. These are the newest ideas in the historic process of adapting schools and colleges to the individual needs of their students. By extending the individualization of instruction to new dimensions, learning contracts provide an answer to endemic problems of every institution: regimentation, irrelevance, and student passivity.

The concept of individualizing educational experiences and centralizing the role of students in the teaching-learning process has characterized all recent major commission studies, including those by the Newman Taskforce, the Carnegie Commission on Higher Education, and the Commission on Non-Traditional Study. All argue for more variety in college programs, for more alternatives in curricula, and for a greater emphasis on meeting the needs of the individual students rather than on prepackaging educational experiences with the assumption that these experiences are right for everyone. Their recommendations are epitomized by the statement from the Commission on Non-Traditional Study, which serves as a continuing theme for this book: "We are talking about an attitude that puts the student first and the institution second, concentrates more on the former's need than the latter's convenience, encourages diversity of individual opportunity, and deemphasizes time and space or even course requirements in favor of competence and, where applicable, performance" (1973, p. 6).

The history of American higher education is replete with examples of prior approaches to individualizing the undergraduate experience. Most famous, of course, is the elective system—ranging from President Eliot's "free elective" plan at Harvard to the more common plans of allowing students to select courses from among a variety within several broad areas such as the humanities or the sciences. Other approaches have included multiple tracking and ability grouping; joint, interdisciplinary, and student-designed majors; alternate paths to meeting specific degree or competency requirements; independent study; directed readings; and individual tutorial. All these efforts have contrasted with the nineteenth century Lancastrian system of mass-producing students through a totally prescribed and regimented sequential curriculum.

urgency for individualized learning

The basic behavioral principle from which all of these efforts at individualization have stemmed is that of individual differences. Students differ so greatly in their personal characteristics—such as their readiness for learning, their motivation for learning, and the amount of their past learning—that institutions will be more effective if they fit their educational programs as closely as possible to their students' individual needs. The psychological evidence supporting this principle has been accumulating for the past 150 years. Recent developments in American higher education have made its implementation more urgent than before.

First, the philosophical basis of American higher education has continued to become more egalitarian in terms of opportunities for more students to attend institutions of higher learning. As a result, the student community is now highly diverse in ability, age, academic and occupational interest, past achievement, and goals for the educational experience.

Second, the entry and the return of students over age twenty-one to higher education has major implications for individualization of instruction, as the idea gains acceptance that schools and colleges are responsible not only for educating the young but also for reeducating the middle-aged and elderly.

Third, the knowledge explosion compounds the question of what an educated person should know. Because of this uncertainty, the task of higher education becomes less the imparting of specific knowledge and more the development of skills and techniques for continued self-education.

Fourth, the growth of external degree programs and the

increased acceptance by many institutions of credit by examination and credit for past learning experiences (over one thousand institutions now grant credit for successful performance on the College Level Examination Program) is likely to increase expectations that institutions will meet the student where he is rather than prescribing educational experiences in a restricted way.

Fifth, many students feel anonymous and helpless because of the large campuses and the heavy reliance on computers and other mechanized processes for registration, record-keeping, and in some cases even advising. These problems deserve attention by colleges and universities if they are concerned with treating students as human beings and individuals.

Sixth and finally, today's eighteen- to twenty-one-year-old students (still the majority of those enrolled in higher education) are about a year more mature, both physiologically and socially, than this age group was a decade ago. They have greater knowledge by the time they enter college, largely because of the pervasive news media. And many of them are "grouped out" by the time they get to college: they have been members of Cub Scouts, Brownies, youth groups, and various organizations throughout elementary and secondary school; they may feel freer to express their individuality during college than previous generations have felt.

As a result of all these recent developments, more and more educational institutions are helping students tailor-make programs to meet their own needs rather than shuttling them through prepackaged sets of requirements.

unique contributions of learning contracts

Among the several means by which colleges can individualize their programs, contracting offers certain unique features. It requires not only student initiative but also student responsibility for goal-setting and goal achievement and student skill at persuasion and negotiation. Unlike most independent study projects, it requires students to formally specify their intentions and plans at the beginning so that their achievement can be assessed with reference to their original commitment. In short, it combines freedom and responsibility in a structured form: if a student wants the freedom to choose what he desires to study, he must also accept the responsibility of active pursuit. As Paul Dressel points out, the contractual procedure is a valuable learning process in itself; apart from the substantive material to be learned, it "helps the student to set his own goals and to be responsible for their realization" (1971, p. 61).

The fact that people learn what they want to learn and what they commit themselves to learn—and therefore the need for student involvement in the selection of learning experiences—represents an idea propounded not only by contemporary educators but by philosophers of earlier centuries. Thus to Socrates and Plato, teachers were mere mid-wives who might help a youth give birth to his soul and yet, in providing such assistance, taught nothing but instead stimulated the youth's memory and perceptiveness. One may recall those lines from *The Republic,* "bodily exercise, when compulsory, does no harm on the body; but knowledge which is acquired under compulsion obtains no hold on the mind" (Plato, 1952, p. 399). In contrast to much contemporary regimented educational practice, the pedagogy of these teachers was based on the conviction that from the beginning the student was inalienably free and ultimately responsible.

The quadrivium and the trivium of the Middle Ages went far in conceiving knowledge to be a fairly fixed body of information permitting little room for student centered experiences; and the impersonal and highly structured curriculum which has characterized most institutions of higher learning until recently has not permitted students a significant role in shaping their curricular experiences. Even when the principle of individual differences has been recognized, it has all too often been used in adjusting different students to a common program rather than in creating the options for students to maximize their own interests and desires.

Learning contracts allow a faculty member to play the role of intellectual midwife and advisor rather than that of parent. Faculty members no longer tell students what they should take; instead, they assist the student with the development and clarification of learning goals, self-understanding, and self-direction, and they evaluate the student's achievement according to agreed-upon measures, rather than taking prescriptive and punitive measures. Contract learning programs necessitate faculty-member concern with the development of students as individuals, not just their cognitive development but also their social and emotional growth.

Contracts, as their name implies, necessitate the agreement of at least two parties—a student and a faculty or staff member or a faculty committee. Most plans expect students and their advisors or mentors to discuss the proposed contract in person before formalizing it in writing. This negotiating relationship with an adult frequently marks a student's initial growth from childhood dependent status to increasingly adult independent status.

Moreover, the learning contract usually begins with the specification of the student's general and immediate educational goals. Students who might otherwise slide through college without ever articulating their goals (as many do) are forced to consider such questions as "Who am I", "Where do I want to go?", "How do I want to get there?" Some students who have entered a contract program after spending a few years in more traditional curricula in other colleges report that it is the first time any faculty member has asked them these basic questions and, often, that it is the first time the students have pursued such questions themselves.

In short, learning contracts attempt to provide individualized flexibility to students, as do other approaches to individualization, while at the same time emphasizing student initiative, involvement, and responsibility in educational decisions, together with advisory support from faculty and other staff members within the academic community and a more adult relationship between students and faculty in considering students' goals and planning their programs.

growth of the learning contract approach

The most recent information available indicates that over three hundred colleges and universities are using learning contracts either for total programs or for particular courses or special types of learning, such as out-of-class and off-campus experiences. These institutions do not usually restrict contracts to any particular time length or discipline, although content and emphasis varies from one operational model to another. For example, one model emphasizes vocational or professional competence as the prime goal of the contract; others emphasize an academic approach either to a discipline or interdisciplinary work; still others take a problem-oriented approach or emphasize an aesthetic learning experience for the student.

Colleges and universities are taking varied routes to the creation of contract learning programs. Some have transformed their total curriculum; others have substituted contract learning as an alternative to various courses; still others have made only minor modifications such as adding the option to contract for grades in existing courses. Because of the diversity in approach taken by different institutions in terms of their distinctive educational missions and their differing clientele, the case studies on the following pages deliberately include a wide variety of full-scale contracting plans. These range from exclusive use of contracts, such as at Empire State and New College, to special units and cluster colleges of traditional institutions, such as at Morgan State, Michigan State, and the University of Alabama. All of them, however, exemplify the concept of students contracting for *learning*, not merely for grades in traditional courses. They illustrate the practical consequences of contract plans, such as enrollments, financial requirements, and changed faculty roles. They indicate the potential that learning contracts have for further individualization of higher education and for an increasing role of students in shaping their own education.

references

Commission on Non-Traditional Study. "Recommendations of the Commission." *The Chronicle of Higher Education,* February 5, 1973, 7 (18): 6.

Dash, E. "Contract for Grades." Washington: ERIC Clearinghouse on Higher Education, 1970.

Dressel, P. L. (Ed.) *The New Colleges: Toward an Appraisal.* Iowa City: American College Testing Program, 1971.

Neal R. Berte is vice-president for educational development of the University of Alabama and dean of its New College, which is described later in this issue. Among his writings, he edited Innovations in Undergraduate Education: Selected Institutional Profiles and Thoughts about Experimentalism *(the University of Alabama, 1972), the report of a conference cosponsored by Alabama's New College and the National Science Foundation.*

*How learning contracts shift authority
from institutions to individuals, as revealed
by three years of experience with the
contract system at Florida's New College.*

learning contracts at
new college, sarasota

james feeney
gresham riley

Colleges, like governments, wield both power and authority. Although closely related, power and authority are really quite different. Power is the ability or capacity to exercise control over others. Authority, on the other hand, is the capacity to control others where the others accept the control as legitimate and proper. Power can always be augmented; authority once lost is infinitely more difficult to restore.

A crisis exists in higher education today because colleges and universities have lost authority. Nowhere is their loss of authority more evident than in the area of curricula. A curriculum can be understood as a college's conception of relevant knowledge and operation of the learning process. Colleges, throughout most of the history of American higher education, have been able to control their students' programs of study, imposing clearly defined conceptions of knowledge.

But during the late sixties and early seventies the prestige of colleges and universities (which supports their authority) suffered serious blows: In the face of complaints from right and left, higher education began to lose claim to scholarly detachment. Young people, liberated by increased wealth, mobility, and the relaxation of many traditional constraints on behavior, increasingly valued working with their hands and participating in the expressive arts—and in attaining "respectability" in ways other than putting in four years at the college of their choice.

The instrumental value of many degrees, particularly those in the liberal arts and the sciences, declined due to "overproduction" of degree-holders and growing employer awareness that possession of a liberal education was not necessarily related to on-the-job competence. The respect once afforded faculty members lessened due to student skepticism of the relevance of knowledge they generate. The cumulative effects of years of growing specialization in the academic disciplines left few scholars who could agree among themselves about what constitutes a liberal education. And students felt an increasing "take it or leave it" attitude with respect to imposed curricula. Consequently, the ability of colleges to operationalize a given conception of knowledge has become problematical.

In their attempt to remain viable, colleges are seeking devices that might restore their waning authority. The contract system of education is one such device. When used as the central curricular strategy, the learning contract focuses predominantly on the student—and on the faculty member. It offers even greater flexibility than the elective system because it is not tied to a classroom, credit-hour structure. Its fundamental departure from tradition, however, is its shift of authority away from the institution, toward the individual faculty member and student. The institution becomes little more than a mechanism for bringing faculty members and students together and for providing the auxiliary services for a recognized academic degree. Whereas formerly curriculum committees, deans, or departments (or all together) legitimized decisions and demands, maintained performance standards, and structured roles, individual faculty members working within a contract system find that they and the students are the final arbiters.

The contract system of education is enmeshed, therefore, in an apparent paradox: It is potential for restoring *institutional* authority in the area of the curriculum, while on the other hand, its functions result in a shift of curricular authority from institutions to *individuals*. What appears on the surface, therefore, as a promising corrective to waning collegiate authority may in operation only compound a difficult situation.

The contract system of education presented here is that of New College, Sarasota, Florida, a coeducational liberal arts college granting the Bachelor of Arts degree. Opened in 1964 as a private institution, New College will become New College of the University of South Florida this July 1 as the result of a unique merger between the college and the State University System of Florida. As an honors college of the University, New College will remain on its Sarasota campus and will be financed by a combination of public and private funds. It will retain its distinctive educational program, with the learning contract system as the organizing principle of the curriculum.

New College adopted its present contract curriculum in 1971, in partial response to the significant decline in graduate school applications by New College students after 1968 and to an increasing student demand for participation in the design of their programs of study and an acknowledgment of the difficulty which faculty members have in constructing a curriculum resting on shared intellectual and pedagogical assumptions.

The central requirement of the new curricular structure is that for each of three ten-week terms in an academic year, a student must formulate a contract with a single faculty sponsor. Working with the sponsor, the student is expected to articulate in the contract both short-term and long-term educational as well as career goals, the specific academic and experiential activities by means of which the goals will be pursued, and, finally, the evaluative criteria in terms of which the contract will be certified as fulfilled. Final certification of student performance is to be made by the sponsor on a pass-no credit basis, and the contract itself, rather than credit hours or course units, is to be the basic ingredient in the undergraduate degree. A bachelor's degree requires nine satisfactorily completed contracts (up to four of which can be pursued in off-campus, field experience projects), four satisfactorily completed independent study projects, and a senior research project successfully defended in an oral "baccalaureate examination." Theoretically, the options for contract design and content are to be completely open, for there are no distribution, language, or other general education requirements in the curriculum.

A detailed explanation of New College's learning contract system can be found in the following excerpt from a document presently used by the college to acquaint new students with the program.

At the time the educational contract was adopted as the

THE NEW COLLEGE EDUCATIONAL CONTRACT

Introduction

At New College we believe that the primary aim of education is to nourish individual growth. To accomplish this our educational environment has a rich array of people and opportunities which can be related to you through a unique curricular device we call the Educational Contract. Your responsibility is to find out about our resources and use the curriculum to facilitate exploitation of them.

Every aspect of the college, from the contract and the nongraded curriculum to the unmonitored dormitories, assumes you will take responsibility for yourself. *You* must reach out into the college community and tap its resources. The traditional "props" of grades, required class attendance, dormitory parietals, and the like are gone. People are here to suggest possibilities and challenge you to new levels of understanding and creativity, but they cannot insure that you will become involved in your own development. Only you can do that. The importance of your own inner motivation will become evident as you confront the challenges in creating a contract.

Each term you are at New College you will join with a faculty member (called your *sponsor*) to design a program of activities for that term. The *contract* is the document which describes the program the two of you desire. At the end of the term your academic standing will be determined by your success at fulfilling the term's contract. Nine successfully completed contracts are normally required for the B.A. College work done prior to matriculation at New College can be considered for credit toward the degree, thereby reducing the number of contracts required.

Your First Contract at New College

First, take a candid look at yourself. Contrary to what you may feel when you arrive on campus and enter a world of strangers, you are here because you have many qualities which you can affirm and use. Much of your exploration and involvement will have an *ad hoc* quality as you set out to create a first term's contract. You will stumble upon resources, happen to meet people who can respond to you, be surprised to find an interest you never knew you had. But the college community does not rely solely on chance; several structures and services exist to help you arrange the contract.

Your *orientation advisor* is a member of the faculty or administrative staff who is specifically designated to be available to you and a small group of your fellow students during the first days of the term. He or she will talk with you about ways your interests and goals can be developed through your academic program. The orientation advisor is available as you proceed through your initial formulation of educational goals and can help you identify a potential sponsor for your contract. The *Dean of Student Affairs* and his assistants will be deeply involved in orienting you to campus life during the first weeks. They are ready to aid you with housing problems, obtaining recreational resources, putting on a social function, identifying resources in town, etc. In addition to serving as general resource people, the Dean of Student Affairs and his assistants, as well as the faculty members residing on campus, are available in personal emergencies. The *College Recorder's Office* is the repository for all academic records including your own. The *Recorder* can help if you have questions about the mechanics of the curriculum and your record. The *Off-Campus Study Office* can help you identify field study resources to be used in the future. Two *course lists,* one for the term you are about to begin and one for the entire academic year, tell what courses faculty plan to offer.

The *Human Resources Guide,* which contains profiles of faculty and staff, will help you know the people in this community, as they describe themselves. Read the *Guide* thoroughly. You will find, for example, that many of us have interests not usually associated with our professional fields. With a personal commitment to explore and thorough use of the above resources, you will have a sound basis for finding a contract sponsor and creating your first contract.

Your Contract Sponsor

Your initial explorations should enable you to identify interests and goals which will shape your academic activities for the coming months. Particular interests and goals will in turn suggest a specific faculty member as a potential contract *sponsor.* Discussion between you and a potential sponsor might be viewed as a process of negotiation. The faculty member will have views on what constitutes valid educational endeavor and what skills you need to achieve the ends you propose. You will have your own views on these matters and out of the dialogue can come a mutual understanding about a contract—a decision to make a commitment and put it into writing, to alter goals, or perhaps to search elsewhere, with other faculty.

Once a contract is negotiated, the sponsor becomes the focal point of your various educational activities. With your sponsor you have the opportunity to develop themes from disparate events, plan for the future, assess the past.

Writing Up the Contract

The contract has four basic parts: Goals, Educational Activities, Descriptions, and Certification Criteria. Below are some guidelines for filling out each part. A sample contract blank is included to aid you in following this discussion.

Goals. This part of your contract is intended to give an overview and unifying theme for your contract. In it you should state long-range and short-range goals, indicating how the term's activities relate to both types of goal. For example, a long-range goal underlying your work might be to have a career in medicine. A short-range goal for a term or series of terms would be to master certain bodies of knowledge which are prerequisite to a medical career. To this end, work in, say, organic chemistry would be included in the term's contract. Not all goals can be so readily expressed in academic terminology as in the example just given.

Educational Activities. This section is for listing the particular activities you intend to pursue as means for attaining your formal academic goals. Because most of the activities you list will be recorded on your transcript by the Recorder, it is important that you understand this section clearly. If in doubt about a particular listing, consult your faculty sponsor and the Recorder. It is very important to differentiate (in the contract) between activities that you are engaging in *for transcript entry* and those which are an important part of your overall program for the term but are not to be entered on a transcript. Only activities planned with and evaluated by New College faculty members will be entered on your transcript. Such activities may be any combination of courses, tutorials, laboratories, field work, and special projects. The course list announces courses and laboratories in advance of the term in which they are offered.

Satisfactory completion of a course, laboratory, or tutorial means that through your work you have met the instructor's performance standards. The instructor will submit an evaluation of your work at the end of the term. Most evaluations comment on the substance of the work to aid you in assessing your academic competence.

In some instances special projects will not be intended for evaluation and eventual transcript listing. Perhaps no faculty member is competent to evaluate the performance involved, or perhaps the activity is highly subjective in nature and an observer's comments are not appropriate. The reason for listing such activities on the contract at all is simply to recognize that they are part of your educational program.

Descriptions And Other Activities. This section is to allow for further elaboration and description of the activities listed above for transcript entry. Normally entries such as courses, laboratories, etc. do not need further description; however, tutorials and especially special projects may require further description. Also, here you may list projects and activities that you are not undertaking for transcript entry but which you and your sponsor consider an important part of your term's study. Activities such as "singing in a madrigal group" and "helping register voters" are examples of endeavors you might wish to note on your contract but which you and your sponsor might not consider part of your formal education.

Certification Criteria. You and your sponsor have complete autonomy over selection of your educational activities and procedures for evaluating your contract. This section of the contract is where you spell out in detail the criteria for satisfactory completion of the contract. The certification criteria for a given contract might be quite simple. For example, they might be satisfactory completion of several or all of a group of seminars you have listed. In that case you have only to attain satisfactory performances as certified by evaluations from the instructors involved. But a contract consists of goals to be accomplished as well as seminars to be completed, and you may want the certification criteria to reflect this. When the criteria for completing a contract are other (or more) than satisfactory completion of a group of faculty-supervised activities, you and your sponsor must be careful to avoid misunderstanding.

Contract Certification

At the end of the term your contract sponsor will determine the status of your contract according to the certification criteria you (both) agreed upon at the outset. In the simplest cases, all the sponsor need do is verify that you have achieved the requisite "satisfactories" in the term's activities. In instances where the criteria for certification are less clear-cut, the sponsor will refer to the conferences you and he or she have had during the term. In every instance you should request a term's end conference with your sponsor to review your progress to date and plan for following terms. Based on the evidence of term's work submitted to her or him, the sponsor will select from three mutually exclusive categories to describe your contract's status: *satisfactory, incomplete,* and *unsatisfactory*. The first means that you have been judged as having met the obligations to which you originally committed yourself. The second, "incomplete," means that you have completed some of the obligations successfully, but not all. When the unfulfilled portions are completed according to a schedule you and the sponsor devise, the status of the contract can be shifted by the sponsor to "satisfactory." However, *a contract not completed within one calendar year from the beginning of the term for which the contract was written becomes unsatisfactory*. Finally, if your sponsor determines that your work is inadequate in major respects and correction of the deficiencies unlikely or educationally unprofitable, your contract will be called "unsatisfactory."

The future is free and open. We look forward
to a year of life, of struggle, and of joy.

central curricular device at New College, fundamental changes were expected in the college's academic program, based on a view of the newly developed contract system as both "open" and "pure." It is "open" in the sense that no restrictions exist with respect to either contract design or content; and it is "pure" in the sense that no curriculum committee or administrator can veto a contract or intervene in any way between individual student and individual sponsor.

In such a contract system, considerable variety was expected among student contracts, but it was less than was anticipated. Nevertheless, interesting differences do exist. In order to highlight these differences and to clarify further what contracting at New College means, we are reproducing sample contracts here. To insure anonymity we have deleted all data which might have served to identify either student or contract sponsor. Furthermore, for analytical purposes we have organized the examples according to types. We do not intend to suggest that this typology is exhaustive nor that all or most contracts would fit neatly into it. Hopefully, by organizing the sample contracts in this manner, the variety that is possible in the New College system will become apparent. The seven types which we have isolated are: the Survey Contract; the Methodological Contract; the Thematic Contract; the Research Contract; the Skill Contract; the Applied Contract; and the Off-Campus Study Contract.*

two years' results

In two years' experience with the contract, dramatic changes were most expected, but have barely appeared in the area of individual program design. Although the contract system encourages students to integrate their curricular and extracurricular activities in relation to educational and career goals, they designed programs that have been, for the most part, highly conventional. The specific subject matter may vary widely, but such variety does not derive from the unique features of the contract system; it comes from a low student-faculty ratio, which allows for tutorials and independent reading programs or study projects. Most contracts consist of a collection of three, four, or more formal courses related to relatively amorphous, short-run goals, with passing work in the individual courses as the primary criterion of success. During the fall

---

*For their assistance in preparing these samples the authors wish to express their appreciation to Dr. Dru Dougherty and Dr. Natalie Rosel.

survey contract

```
                                    __X__  On-Campus
                                    _____  Off-Campus Study
                                    Campus
NAME _____     Box No. _____
```

Goals:

To gain a better basic understanding of many areas of study, and therefore attempt to identify my main areas of interest.

Educational Activities to be evaluated
for transcript entry: Instructor/Evaluator

	Intro. Biology II	
Please have	Intro. Biology Lab	
applicable	Human Economics	
faculty mem-	Intro. to Social Psychology	
bers initial	Social and Political Philosophy	
the following:	Philosophy of Psychology	
Tutorials,	A Study of War—Audit	
Fieldwork,		
Spec. Projects		

Descriptions and Other Activities:

Ballet twice a week (2 hours); jewelry-making twice a week (5 hours); daily flute practice sessions; ceramics.

Certification Criteria:

To complete successfully at least four courses.

```
Student Signature _____   Date _____
Sponsor Signature _____   Date _____
Consultant (when applicable) _____   Date _____
```

18

methodological contract

_____x_____ On-Campus
_____ Off-Campus Study

Campus
Box No. _____

NAME _____

Goals:

As there are only two terms left to my stay at New College, in the time remaining I hope to get experience and knowledge in those areas of biology which I expect to be relevant to my future work in animal behavior. My goals this term are to study, learn and perform the techniques and methods involved in describing as many aspects of an ecosystem as feasible in a term's time, so as to apply eventually the data to a particular problem or problems.

Educational Activities to be evaluated
for transcript entry: **Instructor/Evaluator**

Please have	Bird identification and census.	_____
applicable	Determination of mammal population	_____
faculty mem-	and density.	_____
bers initial	Determination of composition and rela-	_____
the following:	tive density of terrestial inverte-	_____
Tutorials,	brates, including use of appropriate	_____
Fieldwork,	biological keys.	_____
Spec. Projects	Study of life histories of selected ani-	_____
	mals from above studies.	_____
	General knowledge of methods of vege-	_____
	tation and soil analysis.	_____

Descriptions and Other Activities:

These studies will be performed on groups of islands in the Sarasota vicinity. Bird studies will include a count of the number of species seen, number of individuals of each species and the activities the birds engage in. Mammal study will be done with a grid system and capture-recapture techniques. Invertebrate study will include flying, crawling and soil organisms, using a variety of methods. Knowledge of vegetation and soil analysis, as well as other physico-chemical aspects of the environment, will come from working with people studying these areas, assisting them whenever possible.

Certification Criteria:

Certification will be based on competence in techniques and methods learned in all areas of the study and the kind and amount of knowledge acquired in the study. These will be judged by a critical self-evaluation and by discussions with my contract sponsor.

Student Signature _____   Date _____
Sponsor Signature _____   Date _____
Consultant (when applicable) _____   Date _____

thematic contract

```
                                    __x__ On-Campus
                                    _____ Off-Campus Study
                                    Campus
NAME _____ Box No. _____
```

Goals:

I wish to continue my study of Latin America this term. My approach will concentrate on an anthropological approach as well as on the language and literature
of the area.

I will also continue my interest in language and language learning: learning a new
language and teaching two others, as well as studying language from a theoretical
viewpoint.

Educational Activities to be evaluated
for transcript entry: Instructor/Evaluator

	Methods in Cultural Anthropology	_____
Please have	Latin America (Anthropology)	_____
applicable	Women in Latin America	_____
faculty mem-	Latin American Literature	_____
bers initial	Romantics: English Poets	_____
the following:	Beginning Portuguese	_____
Tutorials,	Fieldwork in Bilingual Education	_____
Fieldwork,	Seminar in Linguistics (non-credit)	_____
Spec. Projects	Tutoring in Spanish	_____

Descriptions and Other Activities:

Women in Latin America will be a study of the role of women in that area.
Readings will include a theoretical treatment of sex roles as well as individual
readings on various women, groups, and countries.

Latin American Literature will be a survey of the literature with special emphasis on trends in literature in general.

Beginning Portuguese will be done independently using *Modern Portuguese*
(PLDG) and accompanying tapes. A minimum of 3 hours per week will be
spent in the lab. Fieldwork will be an extension of last term's activities.

Certification Criteria:

This contract will be judged satisfactory by mutual consent of the contract
sponsor and the student, using individual course evaluations as a basis.

```
Student Signature _____ Date _____
Sponsor Signature _____ Date _____
Consultant (when applicable) _____ Date _____
```

research contract

<table>
<tr><td></td><td></td><td> __x__ On-Campus
_____ Off-Campus Study</td></tr>
</table>

NAME _____   Campus
                                                               Box No. _____

Goals:

To develop a full understanding of x-ray crystallography and to solve a crystal structure.

Educational Activities to be evaluated
for transcript entry: Instructor/Evaluator

                        Crystal Structure Analysis _____   _____

Please have   Crystallographic Computer Program-   _____
applicable   ming _____   _____
faculty mem-   Readings in Crystallographic Theory   _____
bers initial   Research in Inorganic Chemistry _____   _____
the following: _____   _____
Tutorials,   _____   _____
Fieldwork,   _____   _____
Spec. Projects _____   _____
               _____   _____
               _____   _____

Descriptions and Other Activities:

Four tutorials with a member of the chemistry faculty. I will be working to achieve the above stated goals and to establish on-campus facilities for the solution of crystal structures.

Certification Criteria:

Satisfactory completion of above to be determined by my research sponsor.

Student Signature _____   Date _____
Sponsor Signature _____   Date _____
Consultant (when applicable) _____   Date _____

skill contract

_____x___ On-Campus
_____ Off-Campus Study

NAME _____

Campus
Box No. _____

Goals:

I would like to become proficient at several classical languages. I also want to study ancient cultures and their arts. I believe that these foundations will assist me in a career in Archaeology, the field of my primary interest. During this term, I intend to remain active in both on- and off-campus activities as well as academic studies.

Educational Activities to be evaluated for transcript entry:

Instructor/Evaluator

Please have applicable faculty members initial the following: Tutorials, Fieldwork, Spec. Projects

Intermediate Greek _____
Latin _____
The Ancient Mediterranean _____
Medieval Music _____
Creative Drawing I: Point/Line _____
_____ _____
_____ _____
_____ _____
_____ _____

Descriptions and Other Activities:

During this period, I intend to do considerable reading in archaeology. At the end of the term I will present an annotated bibliography to my sponsor, listing the reading that I have done. This term I will also continue with my job at the Sarasota Boys' Club as an art instructor. I will also be a sailing instructor on campus. The Latin tutorial will enable me to review my high school Latin and progress into more advanced work.

Certification Criteria:

In order to obtain a satisfactory contract evaluation I will complete four out of five courses in a satisfactory manner.

Student Signature _____ Date _____
Sponsor Signature _____ Date _____
Consultant (when applicable) _____ Date _____

22

"applied" contract

```
                                              _____ On-Campus
                                              __x__ Off-Campus Study

                                              Campus
       NAME _____  Box No. _____
       Goals:
       This term I intend to examine several different aspects of political science. My
       major concern is campaigning for the Constitutional Convention in New Hamp-
       shire. Whatever the results, I hope that this experience will help me in prepar-
       ing for my campaign for the New Hampshire legislature.



       Educational Activities to be evaluated
       for transcript entry:                                    Instructor/Evaluator
                          Revising the Constitution             _____
       Please have        Public Opinion                        _____
       applicable         Tutorial: The Kennedy Administration  _____
       faculty mem-       Special Project: Campaigning for the  _____
       bers initial         Constitutional Convention in New    _____
       the following:     Hampshire*                            _____
       Tutorials,         _____      _____
       Fieldwork,         _____      _____
       Spec. Projects     _____      _____
                          _____      _____
```

Descriptions and Other Activities:
*This will involve going to New Hampshire for two weeks and campaigning
until the election, March 5th. I will report to my sponsor upon my return on
my experiences.
I will be working 15 hours a week as a waitress.
I will be, independently, improving my photographic skills.

Certification Criteria:
Satisfactory completion of three courses and the campaign.


```
       Student Signature _____  Date _____
       Sponsor Signature _____  Date _____
       Consultant (when applicable) _____  Date _____
```

off-campus study contract

```
                              _____ On-Campus
                              __x__ Off-Campus Study
                              Campus
NAME _____  Box No. _____
```

Goals:

To enable each student to better understand the qualities and problems of traditional urban life and, more broadly, to expand personal competence and consciousness by undertaking research and service obligations in a culture different from those we are most experienced in. Toward these basic goals students will employ team research and sharing of urban experience along with the individual activities conventionally involved in a field experience term.

Educational Activities to be evaluated
for transcript entry: Instructor/Evaluator

Please have	1. Internship with an agency or group providing some service in and to Hoboken, New Jersey.	
applicable		
faculty mem-	2. Team research project on some aspect of Hoboken life.*	
bers initial		
the following:	3. "Empathic study" of a Hoboken person, family, work group or the like.	
Tutorials,		
Fieldwork,		
Spec. Projects		

Descriptions and Other Activities:

Other activities: Homestay with a Hoboken area family. Participation in weekly meetings of New College group, some of which will be focused around topics selected in advance of the meetings by participants and taped for use at New College. *Descriptions:* (1) Undertake obligations with community group or agency. One or both of two thrusts will probably develop: undertake an action project for which student has major responsibility and see it through to completion, or carry out a research project providing significant analysis of some aspect of the group's functioning or plans. (2) Study of urban life carried out as a team effort by program participants. (3) Study of a person's or "natural group's" lifestyle and the forces which shape it. The student will project him/herself into the situation of the subject and try to understand the subject's behavior in the subject's terms.

Certification Criteria:

Satisfactory completion of the above-listed "transcript" activities; successful carrying through of a home-stay for the term; participation in the group meetings to satisfaction of the group. There will be a discussion of the term's accomplishments, problems, benefits involving participants and sponsors at end of term.

```
Student Signature _____  Date _____
Sponsor Signature _____  Date _____
Consultant (when applicable) _____  Date _____
```

*The team, not the individual student, will be evaluated. Team evaluation will apply to all team members without differentiation.

term (1973-1974), for example, 303 (62 percent) out of a total 489 contracts were basically of this type. Only 5 percent (twenty-four) of the contracts required a self-evaluation from the student as part of the certification criteria. Yet the contract system was adopted, in part, because it was viewed as a predominantly "student-centered" curricular device. Students or their sponsors (or both) have not responded with the expected self-reflection or inventiveness in program design. It could be that the faculty were not well trained in the use of contracts outside of courses.

The area of teaching techniques has produced as little drama as the area of program design. Most campus work is done through lecture-discussion courses, seminars, tutorials, and independent study. All of these modes were in widespread use toward the same pedagogical ends prior to the adoption of the contract system. One exception to this pattern has occurred in the social sciences and biology, where cross-cultural and field studies now play an important role. The contract system facilitates the design of field-based projects and their incorporation into the formal academic program. Although possibly part of a national trend, students in political science, sociology, anthropology, social psychology, and biology in the New College program increasingly use cross-cultural experience and field research as tools of study. This contrasts with the earlier, more conventional curricular structure, which tended either to discourage field-based projects or to force them into inappropriate molds designed for classroom activities.

The conventionality of contract design and pedagogical techniques under the contract system confirms perhaps the survival potential of the traditional disciplines (including the languages which are well enrolled) in a structure lacking external compulsion. This should be reassuring to those who fear that traditional, widely validated academic activities can prosper only if some formal force, however benign, imposes them on the individual; however, it will probably not be reassuring to those who think that conventional, curricular rules have been the primary impediments to creative student and faculty activity.

Student-faculty interaction, always considered an important dimension of life at a residential, liberal arts college, does not seem substantially altered by the new curriculum. Now, as well as in the early years of New College, the same variety of interaction patterns —some intimate, some distant and aloof—have been observed. This is disquieting because the student-contract sponsor relationship is much more central to the success of the contract curriculum than the student-academic advisor relationship is for a traditional curriculum. In the absence of institutional constraints, a contract system is wholly dependent upon the quality of student-faculty interaction for maintaining program coherence and academic excellence. If the quality of this interaction is marginal, students can, with ease, become casual dilettantes or narrowly trained specialists. While neither extreme has become the pattern at New College, sufficient cases have shown a tendency to move toward either extreme. At one extreme, several students go through much of their college careers without articulating long-term goals, just shifting from area to area and avoiding focus in their programs of study. At an opposite extreme, faculty members can and often do permit students to concentrate excessively in a given discipline or a limited number of disciplines. Thus, we presently have an example of two students with a combined total of eleven academic terms, who have successfully completed thirty-seven courses in mathematics and only eight courses outside this discipline. While these two students provide extreme examples, the phenomenon in question occurs most often in the humanities, not the sciences. The contract system alone would appear, therefore, to be an inadequate response to the problem of the gulf between the "two cultures" of science and humanities.

Finally, innovators generally look to curricular changes to affect a college's admissions and attrition patterns, placing the college in a more competitive admissions position and yielding a better retention rate. Although a two-year period is too brief to allow for definitive claims, New College's shift from a relatively traditional curriculum to the contract system has not had dramatic consequences in these two areas.

In summation, the point to be stressed is that the contract system at New College has not introduced radical changes. It is not the path to a new philistinism—an unleashing of the counterculture —as some have predicted. At the same time, it is not a means for releasing heretofore suppressed student genius which will usher in an educational utopia (see also Hook, 1971 and Waterman, 1972-1973).

limits of the contract system

Why has New College experienced a lack of drama, so little overall change? We believe the answer is that curricular structure, per se, does not impinge directly on the primary forces affecting educational processes. Furthermore, while the contract system is a response to the erosion of traditional curricular authority, it shows limited promise in mobilizing alternative kinds of authority. By itself, it has only limited influence on the manner in which professors organize their disciplines, teach their specialties, and relate to students; it has a limited effect on the decision of a student to enroll or remain at a particular college. The theoretical options that it offers do not necessarily stimulate students or faculty to experiment, to use new resources, or to engage in new learning modes. The actual structure and content of programs of study depend on the individual faculty members who shape and give legitimacy to a student's program, not on the contract system itself nor on the institution. Far from being a revolutionary development, the educational contract can be a highly conservative structure in that it allows existing staff priorities, disciplinary values, and faculty alliances to persist unconstrained. A contract system of education cannot force new learning priorities or new forms of student-faculty interaction.

A contract system such as the one at New College places a premium on the quality of student-sponsor interaction and, in turn, on the quality of faculty members. Recruitment activity and retention decisions take on greater significance than in colleges with traditional curricula. In addition to the usual professional skills, a candidate for the faculty must have such personal traits as a tolerance for ambiguity and uncertainty, sufficient strength to demand high-quality work from students when institutional constraints are at a minimum, and a system of values which provides a basis for distinguishing momentary fads from what possesses lasting educational merit. In the absence of an officially sanctioned curriculum, the integrity of the institution is wholly dependent upon the presence of such qualities among its faculty members.

As for admissions and attrition, specific curricular structures appear to have little to do with them. In addition to obvious factors such as cost, location, religious preference, and parental prohibitions and incentives, it is the general image of a college which affects selection activity. Most new matriculants know little about the specifics of an institution's curriculum, even though they do have a definite image of the school (not necessarily an accurate one). Admissions data at New College indicate that terms such as *experimental, individualized, academic excellence,* and *concerned faculty* figure most prominently in the minds of applicants. This is true not only under the present contract system, but it was also true when the curriculum adhered to a traditional, liberal arts model.

The military draft has far more to do with attrition patterns than does the curriculum. Family pressures, financial conditions, the job market, and youth-culture trends also have significant impact, and all of these are relatively, if not completely, independent of curricular considerations. While a contract system may keep some students enrolled with the lure of receiving academic credit for off-campus activities, these same students may discover more appealing environments in off-campus work than on a college campus. Rather than reducing the attrition rate, a contract system may, at best, merely redistribute it. This, at least, appears to be the case at New College over the past two years.

conclusions

Although the many negative aspects of the use of the contract system need to be understood and noted, New College's two-year involvement with a contract system suggests that this curricular device, through its flexibility and potential responsiveness to student interests, does ameliorate some of the problems associated with traditional curricula. In particular, students look upon their educational experience in personal terms as a result of participating in their own program design. Opportunities for independent research projects during academic terms are increased, and New College has been rescued from the myopia which comes from thinking that the classroom exhausts the educational universe. Finally, the contract system (even with its limitations) does encourage faculty members who are inclined to explore new ways to organize and to present their disciplines. For these and other reasons, the staff at New College continues to be optimistic about the educational contract. Instead of viewing the problems of a contract system as causes for discouragement, we believe that our two-year experience has given us a realistic perspective from which to assess the educational potential of this curricular device.

For those who might be considering the adoption of a contract-based curriculum, some of the important practical considerations to keep in mind are these:
(1) The contract-based curriculum is not a panacea. It does not magically produce student commitment where there has been none,

imaginative teaching where this has been lacking, intimate student-faculty interaction where perfunctory advising has been standard procedure, or increased admissions applications or better retention statistics where these have been on the decline. New College's experience suggests that a contract system of education may free creative minds; it does not create creativity.

(2) People are everything. As platitudinous as this statement may appear, those who are considering the adoption of a contract system are advised to take it quite seriously. As we have argued above, a contract system of education, rather than introducing a new form of institutional authority, shifts curricular authority to individuals, in particular to individual members of the faculty. This shift is most apparent in such areas as the designing of students' programs of study and the maintenance of quality controls within the educational program. Consequently, the nature of a faculty's strengths and weaknesses is all-important. If an administrator or department chairman has doubts about his faculty's ability to perform in the absense of institutionally sanctioned support mechanisms, he should question the suitability of learning contracts for his institution.

(3) A contractual system of education requires a broader range of faculty competence than a more traditional curriculum. In such a system a professor's responsibility extends beyond research, publication, and classroom instruction into the areas of program design, new forms of academic counseling, and the evaluation of nonclassroom learning (such as field internships and cross-cultural experiences). For many faculty members these activities will represent novel demands for which they have received little or no training. Accompanying the new demands are difficult questions about judging faculty competence and the necessity to forewarn faculty members about the increased range of obligations they need to assume in a contract system.

(4) If a college or university has a lack of consensus on the institution's basic purpose(s), the laissez-faire nature of a contract system may bring on irreconcilable dissension. Unless an institution can tolerate the pluralism which a contract system encourages, serious thought should be given to its suitability for that institution.

(5) A virtue of the contract system of education is that, in spite of its being a potentially revolutionary curricular device, it can be relatively inexpensive (in terms of both time and money) to implement New College developed its program in approximately six months

with a grant of less than ten thousand dollars, which proved sufficient to cover special staff and related costs. In contrast, therefore,
to general education programs which must be launched with fully
articulated core courses, contract programs can be started with a
limited amount of valuable faculty and administrative planning
time.

(6) Although start-up costs for a contract program can be relatively
low, there are costs, unique to the contract system, which are required after implementation. Certain administrative expenses in a
contract program may prove higher than in the case of a conventional curriculum—for example, student academic records are more
complex when they involve contracts and narrative evaluations than
when they consist of course registrations and traditional grades.
Consequently, one can expect that the registrar's office will require
both an expanded staff and a new records system. Administrative
and faculty time required for the review of students in academic
difficulty costs considerable amounts of money. At New College,
no faculty committee approaches the time demands required by the
Student Academic Status Committee, the body which monitors the
individual performance of students. A third example of a cost that
is unique to a contract curriculum is related to the need for special
support systems. One such system is an ongoing program of workshops or training seminars in techniques for effective academic
counseling.

(7) Finally, a contract curriculum tends toward solipsism. Common
educational experiences are a rarity; the pursuit of individual goals
is the rule. A college considering the adoption of a contract system
will need to reinforce its supportive, communal, "nurturing" services if a humane environment conducive to learning, however individualized, is to be maintained.

Although the contract system of education is not a panacea,
to have learned in specific terms why it is not permits New College
to make a modest contribution to the ongoing assessment of a
potentially significant educational reform.

references

Hook, S. "John Dewey and His Betrayers." *Change Magazine*, November 1971,
pp. 22-26.
Waterman, A. "Learning by Contract." *Change Magazine*, Winter 1972-1973,
pp. 12ff.

*James Feeney is assistant dean at the Long Island
Regional Learning Center, Empire State College,
State University of New York in Old Westbury.
Formerly, he was the off-campus study
coordinator at New College in Sarasota, Florida.*

*Gresham Riley is provost of New College, where
he has taught philosophy since 1965. The editor of*
Values, Objectivity and the Social Sciences
*(Addison-Wesley, 1974), he is particularly
interested in the role of values in the social sciences
and in models of explanation in these sciences.*

*How contracts can be used to develop intellectual
competence, with examples from SUNY's
non-campus college and student evaluations
of its contract learning program.*

developing intellectual competence at empire state

arthur w. chickering

Empire State College operates through a series of geographically
separated learning centers located throughout the state of New
York. Students receive counseling on admission prior to articulating
their degree program, which describes their purposes and the learning activities they will undertake to achieve those purposes. This
program, which includes information about competence, knowledge, and personal development achieved prior to enrollment, is
submitted to a faculty committee for approval. When approved it
becomes the general framework within which individual learning
contracts are pursued.

In a contract the mentor and student describe plans for learning in more detail than does a typical professor in a conventional
college course, and the mentor designs a much larger part of the

The initial portion of this paper concerning various dimensions of intel-
lectual competence was prepared mainly by John McCormick. The latter draws
on a report from the Research and Evaluation Staff: Ernest Palola, Assistant
Vice-President for Research and Evaluation; Timothy Lehmann, Director of
Program Evaluation; Paul Bradley, Director of Institutional Research; and Dick
Debus, Director of Cost Analysis. It was prepared with the help of Outcomes
Committee members Laurence Lipsett, Lloyd Lill, and Jerry Tomas.

31

student's studies than does a single faculty member in a conventional college or university department.

Because mentors are called upon to advise students outside their specific area of competence, they need to know about other resources for students. These resources may range widely, such as Empire State College learning programs, State University of New York independent study courses, supervised field and work experiences, courses at other colleges and associations and corporations, correspondence courses, museum programs, and some proprietary school offerings.

contract self-inquiry

The following sets of questions were formulated to help students and faculty members develop effective contracts. In terms of long-range plans or general purposes or aspirations:
(1) Do the long-range purposes go beyond Empire State College and attainment of a degree?
(2) Is there an understandable focus for a program of study? Are there clearly stated goals, or is a coherent theme suggested?

In terms of specific purposes:
(1) What is the product of the contract, behavior, a thing, or an effect?
(2) Do the short-term goals or outcomes make sense in terms of the long-range plans?
(3) Is the student equipped to achieve the stated goals within the contract?
(4) Can the college provide opportunity to pursue these goals?
(5) Will other informed observers such as potential employers, accrediting agencies, or other schools understand the expected outcomes?
(6) If consistent with the particular area or discipline, do the specific purposes provide for diversity both in topic and in learning activities?

In terms of learning plan and activities:
(1) Is the learning plan clear to both student and mentor?
(2) Has the whole possible range of learning modes been considered in writing this contract?
(3) Are the activities relevant to contract goals, and are they manageable? Are they the most reasonable for the purposes and for the student?

(4) How clearly are the criteria described? Do they reflect the objectives of the contract? Are they stated so that student, mentor, and any other intelligent person will understand them?
(5) Will the results leave "tracks" that will give an informed outsider an understanding of what the student has accomplished? Will there be concrete evidence that learning has taken place?
(6) Is the evaluation in the contract related to previous and future contracts?

intellectual competence

The most common educational goal of most colleges and universities is the development of intellectual competence or intellectual skills. The objectives of Empire State College are not centered on knowledge for the sake of knowledge, but rather, the improvement of intellectual skills so a student can solve problems, manage his own existence, and learn how to learn. The educator's role is to deliberately bring such skills to the student and thus expand the student's competence. Intellectual skills then become internalized and functional as problem-solving tools.

If the mentor is to help students move through experiences that are deliberately designed to increase intellectual skills, he must specify what those skills involve and how they can be implemented in learning contracts.

Bloom and others (1956) identify and define knowledge and then proceed to outline five intellectual skills: comprehension, application, analysis, synthesis, and evaluation. Taken collectively, these intellectual skills can be seen as the anatomy of cognitive learning. The objectives of Empire State College are not centered on "knowledge" for the sake of knowledge but rather on these intellectual skills because they increase the capacity of the individual to manage his own affairs and to move effectively within his chosen endeavors.

The following pages contain large segments of actual learning contracts, to illustrate ways in which mentors and students are attempting to deal with cognitive learning. In presenting these segments, we recognize that both cognitive skills and learning contracts serve complex functions, and isolated mention of specific skills is not necessarily the mark of an outstanding learning contract. Characteristically, learning contracts tie things together and make explicit connections between and among related activities.

Thus the general format and organization of the following examples have been purposely altered, but their content has been unchanged except to conceal the identity of the three students and their mentors. They do not stand as complete contract statements, but are intended only to illustrate how learning contracts can involve the various dimensions of intellectual competence identified in italics.

assessing learning contracts

One of the problems with most innovative programs in higher education is the lack of significant attempts to assess the learning experiences of the students. While it should be recognized that the Empire State College program does not have a lengthy period to evaluate, there is information available which suggests some of the strengths and weaknesses of this approach to learning.

A 1974 survey of over 250 Empire State students indicated that 46 percent evaluated the learning contract as superior to traditional learning methods, 26 percent rated it "somewhat better," 13 percent considered it "comparable," and only 2 percent deemed it "somewhat inferior." When students were asked about the learning contract's contribution to personal development, 58 percent checked "much more valuable than regular college course," 12 percent checked "a little more valuable," and 12 percent "about the same." More specifically, 86 percent of the students indicated that they were interested by and attracted to the work their contracts called for, 76 percent said that they were challenged and that learning resources were available when they needed them, and 71 percent indicated that they felt confident and competent in relation to the work they were doing. Approximately 65 percent found that they were stimulated and that new worlds were "opening up." A minority of students reported negative feelings about contracts: 13 percent were worried about evaluation, 4 percent were confused and unclear, and 3 percent were bored and uninterested.

Learning contracts pose challenges for evaluation. In answer to the question about whether evaluation done directly by the mentor was satisfactory, 61 percent answered yes, 8 percent answered no, 20 percent were uncertain, and 10 percent gave no response. Evaluation done by others was judged less satisfactory. One evaluative component of many contracts is a log or journal kept by the student. An item analysis of the logs indicates that 35 percent of the students who kept logs used them to record reflections on

General Purposes. As mentioned in my first contract, I wish to find employment in humanistic, community-related jobs. This, undoubtedly, will never alter. To this end, though, and, parenthetically, since my last contract, my immediate goals have become more concrete. I will continue to study for my undergraduate degree but upon graduation I will be seeking employment as a New York State Parole Officer Trainee. I will also be furthering my education part-time either as a law student or as a candidate for an M.S.W. degree.

Specific Purposes. To continue to ease for me the shock of transition from a traditional learning atmosphere to one experimentally oriented such as Empire's. Presumably by the end of this contract I should be completely acclimated to this new mode of learning.

To study the phenomenon of communication from a philosophical, psychosocial, anthropohistorical perspective. Since communication arises from and consists of many forms (language, painting, etc.), there is an extremely copious area open to study. This is conducive to my purpose, for I wish to learn as much as possible about communication (*Knowledge*).

To prepare me for a test I am scheduled to take in the spring of 1973—that of Parole Officer Trainee. Some of my time (at least five hours per week) will be spent on studying for that test (*Knowledge*).

To explore and test any creative, artistic talents I may have and to evaluate myself with reference to these qualities and abilities (*Evaluation*).

To achieve through this area of study a better, more complete understanding of man, thus enhancing my insight and comprehension for later study and work (*Comprehension*).

Learning Activities. I will engage in an intensive self-study program of reading based largely on my interest in communication and on any books my mentor recommends. Following is an example of some of the questions that will be examined: What is the definition of language? Is this definition the same throughout the social science disciplines? Can facial expression, body movement, etc. be considered language? What are the origins of language? Ontogeny recapitulates phylogeny—is this valid for the study of the origin of language? Will man ever be able to bypass vocalization and communicate telephathically? How efficient is communication in general? (*Knowledge, Comprehension, Analysis, Evaluation, Synthesis, Application*).

Creative activities—at least two of the following four activities will be attempted, and, so as to make them worthwhile and not haphazard, mentors with proficiency in these areas will be consulted for guidance and evaluation: creation of three original oil or acrylics paintings (possibly one abstract, one neorealistic, one realistic); creation of four poems in any form dealing with any subject matter whatsoever; creation of a short, short story; use of photographic equipment as an artistic medium (*Communication skills, Synthesis*).

Utilization of any of the mass communication medias in any way possible (perhaps a field trip to a radio or television station) for a clear, more comprehensive understanding of communication in general. The philosophical (What impact has mass communication had on society?) as well as the pragmatic (Which is the cheapest form of mass communication—written, visual, auditory, etc.?) will be explored (*Evaluation, Comprehension*).

Tutorials in photography, creative writing, and/or painting, when and if they can be arranged.

A reading program designed to equip me with proficiency to take the test for Parole Officer. Since the written test will be concerned with testing "for knowledge, skills, and/or abilities in such areas as: working with clients in treatment or counseling situations; human behavior; and social, economic, and health problems and related programs and services," I will be reading and studying material in such areas (*Knowledge, Application*).

In conjunction with preparation for the Parole Officer test, I will participate, when possible, in the Child Care and Counseling Seminar every Tuesday night (*Comprehension*).

Until the middle of January, I will continue to work approximately twenty-eight hours a week as a supervisor for an insurance company continuing to learn about myself, human interaction, and group psychology. After I terminate my employment, I will work part-time in a clerical capacity at an educational institution.

Evaluation: I will submit an annotated bibliography on my readings (*Comprehension*).

I will use a log, diary, or similar device for keeping a written record of my learning activities (*Communication skills*). In this log I will list the items I read, the field trips I take, and any other pertinent material which pertains to my contract on communication. On the basis of this log I will formulate a statement of self-evaluation for inclusion in my permanent record (*Evaluation, Synthesis*).

I will meet with my mentor weekly or biweekly for one or two hours to discuss my readings, activities, and for advice and planning (*Knowledge, Comprehension, Analysis*).

I will submit any of my creative works for evaluation to those competent in evaluating them at the learning center (*Synthesis, Evaluation*).

Written reports dealing with particular areas of study (e.g. psycholinguistics) will be presented to my mentor for evaluation (*Knowledge*).

One of the practice tests for Probation and Parole Officer from the ARCO study guides will be self-administered and results noted. After sufficient time to prepare, a similar practice test from the same study guide will again be self-administered and the results compared. Any weaknesses will be brought to light and corrected by further study. The contract concludes with an extensive bibliography on the nature of language and culture, the psychology of language, and the philosophy of language (*Knowledge, Application*).

General Purposes. To prepare for a career in philosophy, including the further study, the teaching, writing, reflecting, and discussing which this involves.

Specific Purposes. History of philosophy to be taken in the mode of disciplinary history adapted to exemplary history for contemporary philosophy. (*Contemporary Philosophic Thought, Vol. 3 Perspectives in Education, Religion, and the Arts.* Ed. Howard Kiefer and Milton K. Munitz, SUNY Press, 1970, sections on communications and rhetoric.) (*Knowledge*).

Study of fields to include logic and speculative and practical philosophy.

Actualité, to include experiences of conferences, journals, lectures, symposiums, etc.

Study to proceed to point where relation of concepts to philosophical methods is readily perceived (*Analysis, Synthesis*).

Acquaintance with problem of possible relations of speculative and practical is sought. Also some disposition of logic to be made and defended (*Application*).

Some formulation of current issues and interests of philosophers to be made; probably to be developed in connection with choice of graduate school (*Application, Synthesis*). Student and mentor agree to maintain the above assumptions for the duration of first contract.

Learning Activities. Student will pursue general interest in medieval philosophy by reading and reporting on the following works: "Before the Humanities" (lecture); *Aristotle in the West,* (U. of R. B275); *The Spirit of Medieval Philosophy; Reason and Revelation in the Middle Ages; Nominalists and Realists; A History of Philosophy; Gothic Architecture and Scholasticism* (*Knowledge, Comprehension*).

The student will develop specific interest in medieval philosophy by selecting two or more philosophers for intensive examination. One of these will be St. Thomas Aquinas. Student will peruse McKeon, *Selections from Medieval Philosophers* (2 volumes) with study guides provided by mentor to select other philosophers for thorough examination (*Knowledge, Comprehension*).

A trial paper on each philosopher, one to be devoted to "The Cogency of St. Thomas," will be prepared by student and discussed by him and mentor (*Communication skills, Knowledge, Comprehension*).

Student will begin to develop his acquaintance with philosophers and students of philosophy, their locations, predilections, and preoccupations, by examination of journals, attendance at lectures, etc. (*Knowledge, Comprehension, Synthesis*).

As background reading he will report on: J. L. Austin, "Performance Utterances"; G. Drury, "Twentieth Century Philosophy" (lecture) (*Knowledge*).

Student will attend and report on The Sixth Conference on Value Inquiry: Human Value and the Law (*Comprehension, Synthesis, Evaluation*).

38

third example

General Purposes. To continue and broaden his investigation of the second generation of romantic poets, with particular emphasis on Shelley (*Knowledge*).

Specific Purposes. To broaden his travel by extending it to the Continent, where he will visit Spain, Italy, Switzerland, and France (*Knowledge*).

To broaden his study to include consideration of some philosophic and political theorists of the period, with particular focus on the role of women in society, using texts from eighteenth and nineteenth-century Britain and some from twentieth-century America and Britain as comparisons (*Comprehension*).

To concentrate on his writing, both through the extension of his journal and through more formal writing exercises (*Comprehension, Application, Communication skills*).

To initiate a study of Shakespeare, here through reading, which should be extended through viewing and continued reading. He will write about Shakespeare in Learning Contract IV (*Knowledge*).

Learning Activities. Readings [Extensive bibliography appears here, on Shelley, Shelley's friends, politics and women, Shakespeare, narrative fancy, on Spain, Italy, and France, but is not included in this excerpt] (*Knowledge*).

Writings: Student will continue to keep his journal, recording his Continental experiences and comparing them with his British ones. These will be posted to London at regular intervals (*Application, Synthesis*).

He will write a paper on the influence of Shelley on Byron and Byron on Shelley during the Geneva period. This paper will be due by 31 March (*Communication skills*).

Paper three, dealing with politics and women, Godwin, Mary Wollstonecraft, and Women's Liberation will be submitted upon student's return to London at the beginning of May.

Evaluation: The mentor will read student's journal, commenting on it by post. He will summarize his judgments about student's Continental reports in extended tutorial and evaluation sessions in London during May.

Student will write a self-evaluative paper on his return to London.

The mentor will read and comment on the papers which he submits.

Since student will attempt, during this contract period and the one that will follow in England, to concentrate on the development of his ideas in written papers, and he will be attempting to extend and deepen his reading and understanding of British writers of the nineteenth century, he and his mentor will focus on those materials and the writing that he can develop from them (*Evaluation, Synthesis, Knowledge*).

Since he shall be on the Continent for nearly the full duration of this learning contract, his report on his travel will also make for a major portion of this contract and will be the major activity in it.

readings, reactions, and thoughts relevant to their daily lives, trying to put their contract activities in a larger context of their past experience and present circumstances; 17 percent indicated that the log was basically a record of contract activities; another 17 percent described it as a history of their record at Empire State.

When students were asked to list the major weaknesses in the learning contract method, the largest group, 24 percent, wrote "no weaknesses." Significant proportions of students called attention to several major problem areas: 15 percent were bothered by the lack of group exchange; 10 percent mentioned the need for self-discipline; 8 percent felt that they were too dependent on one mentor. Smaller proportions found it difficult to allocate their time well, needed more structure, found contracts difficult to write and resources hard to find, felt they could not explore interests beyond the contract, and that the Empire State program was confused or confusing.

Despite the independent and sometimes lonely nature of Empire State College studies, 33 percent of the students reported some involvement in group studies or workshops. Learning contracts for field or work experiences were used by 57 percent of the responding students. Tutors were used for specialized knowledge and professional advice, and adjunct faculty were used by 19 percent of the students. Among other learning resources, print predominated, with 73 of the 250 students mentioning libraries and 52 noting books and periodicals. Courses at other colleges were used by thirty-four students and considerable diversity was shown in the use of professionals from museums and galleries, community organizations, government, the mass media, and education.

According to questionnaire answers, Empire State College learning contracts appear to call for high-order cognitive processes —synthesis, evaluation, application, and analysis—"almost all the time" or "a great deal": 74 percent of the responding students checked that they had to use synthesis "almost all of the time," or "a good deal"; 61 percent checked one of the two categories for evaluation; 60 percent for application; and 70 percent for analysis. Memorizing either a great deal or almost all the time was reported by only 15 percent of the students; 41 percent said they spent "very little time" memorizing. On a four-point scale, the modal response in all locations was the second highest point ("a great deal") for analysis, synthesis, and evaluation.

In relation to other areas of competence, 47 percent of the

students reported that the college was a major influence in regard to increasing intellectual competence and curiosity while 3 percent said it was not; 35 percent reported increasing job-related competence, while 19 percent said they did not. More than 30 percent said that they were influenced "to a major extent" in regard to affective abilities of self-reliance, self-understanding, and awareness. From 16 percent to 26 percent reported influence to a major extent in clarifying purposes, self-consistency, understanding others, and interpersonal competence. Students indicating moderate influence by the college ranged from 28 percent to 35 percent in all of these affective categories, while those reporting no influence ranged from 9 percent in awareness to 18 percent in interpersonal competence.

In general, then, Empire State College students encounter a situation generally perceived as being less formal, less structured and less "traditional" than most institutions of higher learning. Students who characterize themselves as having clear and certain learning objectives and who do not radically depart from them have overwhelmingly positive affective and cognitive experiences in the Empire State environment; these students view themselves as actively involved in the learning process through the contract method and feel able to pursue their individual goals. Because of the mentoring process, almost half of the respondents perceive themselves engaged in a process superior to that characterized as traditional. These students see Empire State College and the use of the contract learning approach as an important and necessary vehicle for interesting, challenging, and stimulating learning and for confidence and competence in interpersonal skills. They feel the college fosters self-reliance, self-understanding, clear purposes, self-consistency, understanding others, and interpersonal skills. In addition, students express satisfaction with both the process and the outcome of assuming decision-making responsibility by developing their learning contracts.

reference

Bloom, B. S. (Ed.) *Taxonomy of Educational Objectives Handbook I: Cognitive Domain.* New York: David McKay, 1956.

Arthur W. Chickering, author of Education and Identity *and* Commuting Versus Resident Students, *is vice president for policy analysis and evaluation at Empire State College.*

*The process at Morgan State College of how
goals and objectives materialize into
contracts and experiences, with evidence
on the institutional costs of this process.*

contracting in a university without walls program

argentine s. craig

Major changes to established academic patterns can occur only if
reform movements strike out independently, creating alternative
models rather than attempting to integrate into existing ones. University Without Walls (UWW) at Morgan State College is part of
such a reform movement on a national level. It is a program of the
Union for Experimenting Colleges and Universities (UECU), an
association of twenty-nine institutions that have joined to encourage research and experimentation in higher education.

UWW actually began at Morgan State College when King V.
Cheek brought the idea there with him in 1971, when he became
president. He states (1971, p. 4):

> We began with a few assumptions: that higher education had
> to develop some alternative modes of education different
> from the typical classroom structure; that higher education
> should be available to students from sixteen to sixty, no
> matter where they are. We had these reasons: First, cost. The
> cost of higher education is becoming very expensive, espe-

41

cially in the area of capital outlays and faculty costs. Second, need. It became clear in the sixties, and is clear now, that there is tremendous dissatisfaction on the part of students and faculty with the way we are educating our students. And third, clientele. We are directing this concept at continuing education so learning will be available to all ages. The UWW program provides another alternative in education, which should have multiple alternatives because we have a heterogeneous population, to which education should be responsive.

Morgan State's UWW seeks out those who have been traditionally underrepresented in higher education—blacks and other minorities, women, prisoners, veterans, and older students—and operates on an open admissions policy, admitting students who want to learn with the UWW approach. Since 1971, approximately 250 students have been admitted to UWW at Morgan. Of this number more than 50 percent are women, 75 percent are minorities, 70 percent are over thirty, 15 percent are veterans, and 5 percent are prison inmates. More than 50 percent are considered economically disadvantaged. The program stresses competency, based on achievement of learning objectives and performance criteria, individually defined. Individualization of the education process is the core of the total UWW program, conducted in the learning environment of the home, the college, and the world of work, using the resources of the community that can be made available through a range of educational technology.

contracting process

The program attempts to determine readiness for a degree not by counting the hours spent in the classroom or the numerical average of grades received in courses but rather through completing learning contracts that are reviewed during three evaluation sessions. The process begins at the point of admission with an assessment of the student's document of prior learning experiences (a five-page form that asks questions dealing with past employment positions and skills, other experiences relevant to educational objectives, such as college courses, workshops, conferences, and travel, and personal growth). Through this document the student communicates what she has learned and how it is related to her goals. The program staff assists her in identifying and clearly documenting relevant learning. Staff members with adjunct advisors and outside examiners assess the learning experiences presented in the document. Then the student begins to negotiate her educational experiences, based on her value system; clarification of goals and concepts of what is worth knowing evolve from this process.

At these assessment sessions, questions are raised (for consideration, not necessarily for answers), regarding goals and objectives. For example, if the student's decision is to acquire, in an independent way, a well-rounded liberal arts background before delving deeply into a particular field, options are offered that look something like the example on page 44.

For each learning experience, including regular courses, a learning contract is developed that specifies the experience to be acquired and carries a commitment of written evaluations by the student and her adjunct advisor. The student also documents all of her learning experiences in a journal, which serves as another evaluative tool.

The contract presently used at UWW/Morgan State was adopted in February 1973. Questions raised are: What specific behaviors will you be able to demonstrate as a result of this experience? What content, topics, specific subareas of interest will you explore during this experience? What learning strategies will you use to achieve the stated objectives? How do you know when you have mastered your objectives?

One student developed a twelve-month study program which stipulated an immediate goal as a personnel manager and a future goal as a lawyer. She developed contracts in the following areas: community internship with legal aid bureau to obtain experience in helping to relate to people (twelve-month contract); internship with personnel placement office (six-month contract); regular coursework in personnel analysis and personnel management (a one-semester contract); weekend workshops in personnel management to include sensitivity training (four times a year); an educational television course in management principles for two nights a week (three-month contract). The variety of learning experiences she selected is consistent with one of the UWW program objectives, "to provide a wide range of learning resources . . . so that students have the opportunity to discover the many ways to learn."

The contract developed for the initial internship is outlined on page 46.

44

Traditional Requirements in General Education	Options for Acquiring General Knowledge via UWW Learning Contracts
50 credits in general education distributed among five areas:	*Independent study* resulting in performance competencies demonstrated by the passing of proficiency examinations or the CLEP tests of the College Board; and/or *interdisciplinary seminar* (participation in weekly three-hour seminar for a 12- to 24-month period); and/or *assessment of knowledge* acquired through life experiences; *development areas* (the following can also demonstrate competency and academic scholarship):
(1) English Composition	(1) Journal (maintenance of a daily journal throughout enrollment in program); written self-evaluations for all contracted learning experiences; and projects, internships with newspapers or magazines, written work related to overall developmental plan.
(2) Social Sciences	(2) Independent study (directed readings in the fields of sociology, psychology, anthropology, political science and education; educational television courses in the field of social sciences; and/or internships (see *UWW Directory of Learning Resources*).
(3) Humanities	(3) Independent study (directed readings in the field of Humanities); educational courses (drama, seminars in the arts); and/or travel/study projects (home or abroad to study other cultures and life-styles).
(4) Natural Sciences	(4) Scientific projects in ecology, drugs, nutrition, hypertension; written reports (review of the literature, writing abstract of scientific studies of society); work experience or internships with agencies involved in scientific work; educational television courses (biology, environment, astronomy, spectrum series—field studies that are now under the auspices of leading world scientists from a Moscow operating room to a physics laboratory at Johns Hopkins University);* laboratory experiments (portable minilab from the Open University).

*The rationale and objectives for the traditional science requirements are interpreted by UWW to be for: (1) the development of an understanding of scientific inquiry and critical thought, and (2) the integration and application of scientific principles to solve societal problems.

Traditional Requirements in General Education	*Options for Acquiring General Knowledge via UWW Learning Contracts*
(5) Health and Physical Education	(5) Participation and membership in a health/physical education activity with the Y's, Scouts, Little League, neighborhood recreational groups; informal recreational activities with family, friends, neighbors (bicycling, jogging, tennis, golf, swimming, etc.); personal health program for physical fitness and athletic skills.

46

Title of Learning Experience: University Year for Action Internship: Legal Aid Bureau

Date: September 1972 to September 1973.

Objectives: To be able to demonstrate the technique of interviewing and screening clients to determine the nature of the problem and whether or not a client is eligible for legal aid services.

Learning Activities: Codes of law governing the city of Baltimore and state of Maryland; contents of textbook (*Business Law* by Ronald Anderson); attendance at court hearings to learn that process; and, in some cases, attendance at hearings in the place of an attorney.

Learning strategies: Readings, lectures, consultations with the bureau's lawyers, research (collecting data to prepare cases for court).

Evaluation: When I can work totally independently at Legal Aid on various cases, from beginning to the court; when evaluations from the attorneys at Legal Aid are good; when I am able to discuss various areas of law intelligently.

This was a valuable learning experience for the student because she was contemplating going to law school. By working on a daily basis with lawyers for an entire year, she was exposed to the laws she was reading about and saw them applied to help poor people to solve their problems.

When the advisor made a field visit to the student's internship site, the supervisor (an attorney) indicated that the student was serving as a paralegal professional advocating cases. He stated, "She communicates with lawyers on cases, reads up on laws and attends workshops, interviews clients and classifies problems, works on preparing cases for court and keeps up correspondence with clients." The advisor noted that the student has "great social awareness and involvement in community; feels accomplishment working with people."

One of the contracts referred to in the letter from the student was on psychological statistics, which she developed as shown on page 48.

The contract was a four-month one and at the end of the contracted time, the student had this to say about the learning experience:

> I elected to take this course because I felt that it would help me in my job of preparing reports and statistical tables on the training activities of 250 people in HEW. I needed to be sure I was selecting the appropriate method of data collection and to prepare this information so that it could be easily interpreted by high officials in the organization.
>
> I have learned from this course that statistical data on the career progression of employees must be of a sophistication that will sell the program. I have learned to identify the appropriate method for preparing reports and statistical tables by going through many exercises with the methods listed.
>
> When I started this course I had to develop a personal time schedule for adequate time to devote to the homework exercises. I also felt a knowledge gap in algebra and geometry, which I had taken more than seventeen years ago. Nevertheless, I was determined to overcome this gap by going to the instructor for coaching during his free periods and getting further tutoring from a senior statistician on the job. When difficulties arose concerning the terminology, I decided to

What specific behaviors will you be able to demonstrate as a result of this experience and under what situations? To collect, organize, analyze, and summarize data on my job when preparing reports and statistical tables on the training activities of 250 people in HEW.

What content, topics, specific subareas of interests will you explore during this experience? Frequency distributions, percentile ranks, measures of central tendency, measures of dispersion, normal distribution, standard scores, research methods, Pearson product moment correlation, biserial correlation, Spearman correlation, phi correlation, tetrachoric correlation, sampling theory, T-test for related samples, T-test for independent samples, chi-square test of independence.

What learning strategies will you use to achieve the objectives stated? Develop schedule for homework. Seek counseling from instructor. Seek tutoring from statistician.

How do you know when you have mastered your objectives? I will be able to identify appropriate methods for preparing reports and statistical tables.

What texts and collateral readings will you use? Fundamental Research Statistics by John T. Roscoe.

take my cassette tape recorder to class and tape the lectures so that I could replay the lesson on the way home from work and while traveling to school. This technique worked wonders for me, as I was able to synthesize this highly technical information. . . . I have mastered the subject by the learning techniques mentioned and am able to select the best method for preparing reports.

contracting costs

Helping a student to develop her goals and create learning contracts to reach those goals takes many hours of staff and adjunct advisors' time. Financial resources are needed for student goal development and enrollment and for staffing. For example, before a student's assessment session, she has been given a personal interview of approximately two hours, during which time she is encouraged to write down the past experiences that are relevant to her present goals. The assessment session itself usually takes two hours and involves at least three persons. Conferences of one to two hours are scheduled to create contracts for desired experiences. If a student is interested in developing six contracts per year, the time involved could be four to six hours. Since the contract usually is between the student and a person other than a UWW staff person, additional time is needed for the student and the adjunct advisors to confer. Students meet with their advisors on the average of twice a month for at least one hour per meeting. Adjunct advisors are usually paid five dollars per hour; outside examiners get ten dollars per hour; and program advisors (staff) earn approximately six dollars per hour. Thus, advising costs (in gross figures) amount to approximately $636 per student per year, based on:

2-hour personal interview (advisor, $12; staff, $12; volunteer)	$ 24
2-hour assessment session (advisor, $12; adjunct, $10; examiner, $20)	42
6 contract conferences @ $6 (UWW program advisor)	36
6 contract conferences @ $5 (adjunct advisor)	30
24 individual conferences among 3 adjunct advisors 72 @ $5 per hour)	360
24 individual conferences with program advisor ($6 per hour)	144
	$636

The above model is an "external" type that is workable for the student who does not use any college facilities or resources (regular classes) but is studying independently with the help of advisors and the resources of the city. Income realized would be $159,000 (250 times $636); advising costs would amount to $150,000.

Expenses can also be kept at a minimum in the model that utilizes college facilities and resources. For example, if a program advisor spends approximately thirty-six hours (interview, assessment, individual conference) with each student, having 1920 hours (40 times 48) available for that period, she would be able to advise approximately fifty students. The program would need five full-time program advisors at a total cost of sixty thousand dollars. If a student has three contracts and relates to three adjunct advisors during the year, the program would need 750 adjunct advisors. If each met with her student two hours per month and were paid five dollars per hour, it would cost the program ninety thousand dollars for adjunct advisors' services. The total advising cost to the program would amount to $150,000.

In addition, there are the vitally needed services of secretaries, clerical workers, and administrators to handle and process the written evaluations, contracts, and the paperwork attendant to narrative transcripts and other personalized services characteristic of a coordinated nontraditional program. These noninstructional personnel positions would require approximately forty thousand dollars. Add five thousand dollars more for office supplies, materials, equipment; sixteen thousand dollars (8 percent for overhead) to provide for office and conference space, utilities, janitorial services. The expenses are now approaching two hundred thousand dollars, which may not be prohibitive in light of overall program operation with the outcomes of a quality program based on learning contracts.

Thus the contract model as described may cost no more to operate than the traditional educational program. With the aim of developing a self-supporting program, the cost to the student (at UWW/Morgan State) for fiscal year 1974 is only $824.50 for a twelve-month learning program ($325.50 per semester and $173.50 for the summer session), yielding an income of approximately $206,000 ($824.50 times 250 full-time students), which is adequate to meet the expenses as outlined.

In practice, UWW at Morgan State had an operating budget

for fiscal 1974 of over $200,000, with $118,000 coming from federal sources and the remainder from UWW student tuition and fees. The low cost to the student is consistent with the philosophy of offering educational opportunity to a wider constituency. Such a low cost is possible because of the volunteer services of many adjunct advisors, such as community people, heads of departments in industry, M.D.'s at hospitals, Ph.D.'s at other institutions, supervisors at work stations, teachers in the public and private school systems, newspaper editors, artists, musicians, the Morgan State College faculty, and so forth. In short, an incalcuable contribution is made in terms of human resources. Additionally, the college provides some facilities and services (space, electricity, heat, accounting reports) out of the 8 percent indirect costs from the federal grants. Moreover, students can register for and attend regular courses offered by the college and other state colleges at no additional charge beyond their payment of full-time tuition or fees.

These are the practical realities of the financial factors which require creative use of existing resources to support innovation. Samuel Baskin of the UECU has stated that "The most important feature of UWW is the degree to which we are able to help develop in people a new faith in their own resources—their own potential. . . . If our graduates are able to look to themselves (instead of being dependent on others) for answers, then UWW would have made a difference" ("University Without Walls," 1973). The existence of 250 UWW students at Morgan State and at least 3000 UWW students across the United States affirm that UWW has made a difference. This writer predicts that by 1984 thousands more in hundreds of institutions of higher learning will discover the difference in being free to learn on their terms.

references

Cheek, K. V. *Baltimore News American*, October 1971, p. 4.
"University Without Walls." *Northeastern Regional Newsletter*, Summer 1973, *1* (3).

Argentine S. Craig directs the University Without Walls program at Morgan State College described in this article as well as the Urban Regional Learning Center for the Union for Experimenting Colleges and Universities. Earlier she administered the widely-heralded Parkway Program for the Philadelphia school district, after serving as a teacher-coordinator in Philadelphia's school-work program in distributive education. In her spare time she is working on a book on a bicentennial review of innovation and Black education from 1776 to 1976.

*Examples of field studies, independent studies,
and field education contracts, all demonstrating the
use of contracts to integrate theory and practice
and to help students learn how to learn.*

out-of-class contract learning
at justin morrill

john duley

Learning contracts play a significant role in three basic out-of-class learning opportunities at Justin Morrill College: the *field study* program, a term of off-campus cross-cultural learning, individual *independent study* in a particular discipline, and a *field education* course in which a group of students undertakes a project in the community under the direction of a faculty member. Three kinds of contracts are used: (1) The field study contract focuses attention on the developmental and cross-cultural dimensions of learning and the cognitive dimension is dealt with indirectly or as a derivative of the learning experience. (2) The independent study contract concentrates attention on the cognitive, discipline-oriented dimensions of learning, with indirect attention to the developmental and cross-cultural dimensions. (3) The field education contract is developed by a faculty member or a group of students with a faculty sponsor, with educational objectives that relate to the discipline and the needs and interests of the students.

These offerings differ in design, but they are undergirded by a common set of philosophical convictions. The central conviction at Justin Morrill is that learning is most humane and effective when the student is given as much responsibility as he is ready for to design, develop, and execute his own learning experiences. Sufficient structure is provided to insure rigorous reflection, quality work, and mutual accountability between learner and teacher. Under these circumstances a student is expected to learn to acquire, evaluate, analyze, and synthesize information, to think critically, develop creativity, and be able to continue learning on his own, better than under circumstances in which students' learning is predetermined.

The college program also rests on a belief that it is important for students to experience the direct linkage of theory and practice by practical experience. We provide the educational structures in which students have the opportunity to become "street smart" as well as "book smart."

The educational opportunities for the application of theory in practice, for building bridge experiences to adult roles and for the balancing of our strong intellectual tradition with cross-cultural learning may be best provided by the imaginative and responsible utilization of the larger educational environment of the social, economic and political structures beyond the classroom. A viable means of linking together systematic cognitive learning, the student's personal growth and development and significant involvement in the public realm which we have developed has been the combined use of contract learning and out of class learning. A contract is understood in this context to be a mechanism for agreement between a teacher and a student or a group of students for the purpose of individualized learning within the expanded learning environment available outside of the classroom. It has been found at Michigan State that each contract needs to include the following elements: (1) A clear statement of the purposes of the project including what the student intends to learn and what he hopes to accomplish in or for the community; (2) A description of the project and the means the student plans to use to carry it to completion; (3) A description of the "out of class" resources which the student will be using and the nature of the involvement in the community which the student will have; (4) A description of the various means which will be used for evaluating the student's work.

field study

The field study contract arises out of the necessity to fulfill a college requirement that each student spend a term involved in cross-cultural learning. We contract with him to accept any project he arranges, which fulfills the following criteria: (1) The project must provide for in-depth involvement in a foreign culture, a sub-culture in this country, a new role for the student, or a new social setting unfamiliar to the student, in which he will not be a casual visitor but an active participant in the daily life and affairs of that social environment; (2) the project must be at least nine weeks in duration; (3) if it is in a foreign country, the student must have a two-year competency in the language or be willing to attain such competency prior to going on the project; (4) arrangements must be sufficiently finalized before a staff member will permit a student to enroll for credit. In the event that it is unclear whether or not the project will meet these criteria or can be finally arranged before departure the staff member enters into an agreement with the student to review the project upon the student's return and if it did fulfill the criteria and the student fulfilled the other elements of the contract, he is permitted to enroll for credit and to participate in the follow-up seminar.

The range of options from which a student may choose in arranging his project include: (1) Cross-cultural learning; (2) Occupational exploration; (3) Pre-professional experience; (4) Social action involvement; (5) Service-learning internship. The negotiation of this contract is completed by the end of the term in which the student takes the preparation seminar by his submission and our acceptance of a detailed description of the project for which he had completed the arrangements, a statement of his personal objectives in undertaking this project, his hopes and expectations in regard to the experience. Because of the diverse nature of the projects represented in each preparation seminar, the desire to encourage self-initiated learning, and the differing levels of preparedness of each student, another learning contract is used for the work each student does during the last five weeks of the preparation seminar.

The range of projects in which students engage includes established group programs that require very little initiative on the part of the student, such as those conducted by the Volunteers for International Development or the Experiment in International Living, to individual projects designed and executed by the student, such as that of the student who was a participant/observer with the revolutionary left in Ireland or the experience of four students who purchased, reconditioned, and sailed the *Neith,* a 1908 Herschoff-designed fifty-three-foot sailing ship, from Falmouth, England to Palma, Spain and Antiqua in the Caribbean Sea. These projects also include more moderately demanding experiences, such as serving as

56

a volunteer in an orphanage in Honduras or teaching English as a second language in Mexico City.

A premedical student developed a contract in which he spent his field study living with families and working as a paraprofessional with two general practitioners in two economically different areas of the state for equal periods of time. The doctors were very different: One was an older man with an established practice, who conserved his psychic resources. The other was a young man with a very sensitive social conscience, who spent himself without counting the cost to his personal health or family relationships. Besides developing cross-cultural learning skills, the student confirmed his interest in medicine as a profession, and upon his return to campus, he became deeply involved in the medical work of the Drug Education Center and became a trained counselor in the local Problem Pregnancy Counseling Program. This service involvement was, according to his final paper, the direct result of the field study experience. The contractual nature of this program made this unique placement possible and built into it the reflection which lead to his service involvement.

The crew of the *Neith,* referred to earlier, took an agonizingly long time to complete their contract because of their difficulty in conceptualizing what they knew to be extremely important learning for them. They wrote in their final paper:

> We confronted our Mediterranean situation, and it became very apparent that we could not fulfill our original Michigan State study agreements. They were to be highly structured sociological, anthropological, and geographical investigations of cities adjoining the harbors we visited.* Our actual problems, as opposed to these scholastic ones, were omnipresent and left time for little but their solutions. Realistically, our nautical-type environment required that we direct our total efforts towards survival. The cities for us became sources of food, fuel, supplies, equipment, and repair facilities. In short, they were tools to be used to help replenish the self-contained systems which were necessary for our survival.
>
> In Palma we worked constantly, and the *Neith* was

*Because they were to be gone more than one term, they developed some independent study contracts in addition to their field study contracts.

brought successfully to a high level of readiness. As the months of August and September passed, we began to take more pride in the *Neith* as she neared "yacht finish." She became more and more seaworthy as her systems (lighting, propulsion, protection, communication, maintenance, etc.) were brought up to their maximum possible level of performance. With her increased sea capabilities she would be able to control or divert the energies encountered in most foreseeable circumstances.

On November 28, 1970, we set sail for "the land of the free and the home of the brave." Twenty-eight days would pass prior to our next landfall. The first twenty days of the 3500-mile passage were slow, sunny, and easy. During the frequent periods of calm, we read books and swam under the hot tropical sun. This became the most significant part of the trip. During it we each realized an immense potential to our individual awarenesses and capabilities. This discovery, which was undeniably the most important of the trip, was a collective one. We all enthusiastically discussed it, how the previous nine months of hard work and self-discipline naturally snowballed to this point. Our specialized environment demanded and exercised the full spectrum of our potential. Although many books were read at this time it never bore any resemblance to a "scholastic" learning experience. The effect of the boat was to bring forth full access to all previous experience. The most comprehensive books we had thus far read in our lives were absorbed while being able to interrelate all previous knowledge immediately. The phenomenon was so astounding that we came to the conclusion that this must be what passes for "higher consciousness."

In this state of mind great things seemed possible. It was as though we could comprehend the accomplishments of great men, because we were looking from the same hilltop. Unexpectedly, people widely separated by time, place, and disciplines were found to be united by foundations. Comprehensiveness gave rise to immense energies, and it no longer seemed a mystery how major works were accomplished. We were still isolated in the Atlantic and wondered to each other if what was happening could be brought back into the world we had left a year before.

The change we encountered upon returning to school

was much less of a problem than we had anticipated. We had been told to expect a shock upon reentering college life, but it surprisingly did not occur. The college routine seemed like a pleasantly simple game from what we had left. We realize now why this was true. Other people with field study experiences became more specialized in coping with their study environments. They merely had to discover where and how to plug themselves into static existing environments. Upon return they found it difficult to change from one specialized way of life to another. In contrast, our trip led to a more generalized and comprehensive dynamic understanding, which enabled us to cope with the static, specialized environment we returned to.

One of the crew summed up this change in their way of thinking in this way. "One of the most important single things I have learned after sailing eleven thousand miles is the concept of 'comprehensive thinking.' I describe it as thinking of a system as a whole rather than as a group of separate parts. In this way, I seem to get a view of the entire scope of a particular problem, not just any one aspect; it is the discovery of the underlying fundamental principles which gives me a total outlook on a situation." In that paper he goes on to explain the profound effect that has had on his life and work.

A student who had no clear occupational goals or much sense of direction in her life, as is true of many students, arranged a field study in a settlement house in Liverpool, England through the Winant Volunteers. According to her journal and her final paper she spent most of the first part of her time in Liverpool bitterly complaining to herself and others about the family she lived with and the way they treated her, about the incompetence of the man she worked for, and about the bad condition of the center and its facilities. She was prevented from doing or learning very much by her very negative, fault-finding attitude.

In the course of her third week there she ran into a young American woman who had lived in Liverpool for three years and was working in a youth program which she and some English young people had created. They were living from hand to mouth to keep it going. This meeting influenced the student to quit complaining, link forces with these people, and do a remarkable piece of work in the settlement house she was serving.

In the follow-up seminar she showed a serious reentry problem; she had struggled for a long time in Liverpool, wondering if she ought to stay there. On her return to Justin Morrill at Michigan State she discovered how much it had meant to be needed, counted on, and responsible to and for other people, as she had been for the first time in Liverpool. At Michigan State she rediscovered that it did not matter to anyone whether she was there or not or whether she did anything or not. The experience she contracted for and the reflection built into the contract forced her to do some deep and hard thinking about herself, the influence of her attitudes on her behavior, her values and what she wanted to do with her life. It also demonstrated to her that she could function effectively under strange and adverse circumstances, giving her more self-confidence than she had before.

field experience within a discipline

The second and third type of out-of-class contract learning, independent study and field education, are related to the process of field experience within a discipline. Learning experiences occur in the field in which the scope, language, concepts, assumptions, theories, methodologies, and knowledge of various disciplines is learned and utilized in relation to the consideration of a specific issue or topic in the field. There are three distinctive elements of this out-of-class contract learning experience: (1) The work done in the field is related to a discipline; (2) the work is done under the supervision of a faculty member who is a representative of that discipline; (3) the student's work is accepted for credit on the basis that it demonstrates the knowledge or mastery of an aspect of the discipline which was contracted for by the student and the sponsoring faculty member.

Independent Study. Descriptions follow of two different uses of independent study contracts:

The first deals with two different courses, Politics 1970 and Politics 1972, which are programs focusing on the American electoral process and involving seminar and field experiences. The objectives of the programs are that each student demonstrate (1) an understanding of the electoral process through involvement in it; (2) an understanding of the impact of the political issues of the campaign on the candidate and the electorate; and (3) the ability to use the methodology and insights of political science through an analysis of the trends and possibilities of the election. The objectives are defined by the instructor, with students developing individual contracts for meeting the objectives. The individual contracts detail the specific means by which each student agrees to an involvement in the subject matter and in the political process. Students are encouraged to include direct involvement within a political campaign in their contracts either at the local, state, or national level and in whatever aspect of the campaign they wish to be involved. Each contract includes a component based on the totality of the experience in which an analysis or interpretation of the experience demands an interaction between the affective and the cognitive dimensions. Evaluation is based on demonstrated evidence of the student's involvement in the political process and understanding of the discipline of political science. Throughout both programs, the faculty monitor remains in close touch with the students, utilizing the seminars to provide information and the opportunity for students to share with and to assist and encourage one another.

The second example of an independent study contract was carried out by a number of students while doing their field study in a different cultural setting. They developed independent study contracts in order to study selected aspects of their field study environment, utilizing the concepts and insights of a particular discipline. These contracts are developed in detail and include some work in preparation for the field involvement. The student is expected to demonstrate some mastery of the concepts before departure, since the supervisor is not available in the field. It is understood, however, that the experience itself provides the means for further clarification and verification of the concepts at issue. Effective use of this model has been demonstrated by students focusing on the processes of political and economic development in such countries as Columbia, Greece, Brazil, and Tanzania. Variations have permitted contracts in the process of community development within the Model Cities programs of Lansing, Michigan and Atlanta, Georgia.

An analysis of the effectiveness of the independent study contract indicates that it enables students to pursue their individualized interests and encourages them to a high degree of motivation and interest. Many faculty members have made these learning experiences high points in the academic experiences of students by their mutual involvement with the student in his creative struggle to master some aspect of a discipline in the accomplishment of a clearly defined and specific task. The excitement graduate students and their faculty mentors experience on the frontiers of knowledge are often mirrored in the undergraduate's independent study experience under a wise, sensitive, and creative faculty sponsor.

In the experience of the College, too many independent study projects receive grades of incomplete. Many of them should never have been undertaken, either because they were too ambitious in contract design, setting up objectives which could not be accomplished within the time constraints of the study, or the student was not trained enough in the discipline or experienced enough in working independently to carry out the project or the faculty had insufficient time to provide the necessary support system for the student. More viable contracts would be designed and responsible relationships established between students and sponsors if a college review committee were established to approve all Independent Study projects which are for six or more credits. This would provide a framework for consistency of quality and protect faculty from their tendency to over extend themselves in responding to the individual requests of students.

We have done no research comparing the effectiveness of independent study in the field with classroom learning, but it is clear that contracts are very effective facilitators of learning when the project is of limited enough scope that it can be accomplished through the given skills of the student in the time available, when its objectives are clearly stated, and when the process by which the student is going to complete the project is carefully developed with and monitored by the sponsor.

Field Education or Group Projects. Two examples follow of field education or group contracts. In the first, the initiative for the project came from a group of several students, encouraged by a County Mental Health Coordinator. The purpose of the project was to investigate the apparent disproportionate use of funds among the three counties participating in joint programs. In a meeting with the official and the students, the faculty sponsor agreed to supervise the project, provided it was expanded to include a study of the decision-making processes at the tricounty level regarding mental health programs, with an analysis of possible adjustments in those processes under pending revised revenue-sharing programs. The original project failed when the initiating students did not enroll for credit. Several new students agreed to contract within the suggested objectives for a parallel experience. The resulting contract was between these students and the faculty sponsor, with a further expansion in the frame of reference. The students desired to examine the state legislation, undergoing revision at that time, which authorized and controlled county mental health programs. They agreed further to interview state legislators, county commissioners, mental health board members, and county coordinators and directors before filing a report. The project became a study of intergovernmental relations in the area of mental health.

In the second example of a field education project, a faculty member received a request from the Director of the Model Cities Program of the City of Lansing to assist his staff by finding out for them the levels of understanding and commitment of the various publics involved in the Model Cities Program. Two faculty members responded to this request by initiating a field education project. Twenty-two students were involved in the program as an introduction to political science in the context of urban development. The central core of the course was a survey of the understanding and attitudes of community leaders and participants concerning the Lansing program. The first phase involved the students in a process of identifying influential community leaders. A special team of students surveyed a random sampling of Lansing citizens from business, labor, industry, education, religion, social services, and the mass media. From the initial survey, the persons mentioned most frequently as influential community leaders were interviewed to find out what they knew of and felt towards the Lansing Model Cities Program. Along with these thirty-five identified community leaders, seventeen members of the policy board of the program, one city councilman, and eighteen elected members of nine task forces were interviewed. Three parallel questionnaires were developed by the students for interviews. A final report of the findings of the class was developed and submitted to the director of the program for use with his staff. The execution of the course required the students to find out about the enabling federal legislation establishing the Model Cities Program and to learn about intergovernmental relations as they are expressed in federal, county, and municipal cooperation in programs like Model Cities.

conclusion

There is a persistent restlessness among educators with the model of undergraduate education whose main components consist of a fixed amount of time spent in an institution—time used in rather rigidly predetermined ways, primarily in blocks of eleven or sixteen weeks. In this time, the student is expected to master the content of certain subject matter areas and demonstrate retention powers and thought processes in a narrow way—a final exam. Despite its limitations, this process has served society well. A number of people have learned to learn by means of this process and the ongoing work of our society is carried out by those educated in this way. The current concern of educators is to improve the system so that the main purpose of a liberal education and the use of its resources and talents can concentrate teaching people how to learn and launching them on an ongoing life of inquiry.

Out-of-class contract learning has wide implications when one considers that the concern for lifelong learning goes far beyond serving those who wish to complete their formal education to a certain level. Any program of individualized learning, especially when related to clearly defined interests, would benefit from the use of contracts in the design of the learning experience.

John Duley is assistant professor and director of the Field Study Program of Justin Morrill College at Michigan State University. He is also project director for the University's pilot competency based Liberal Arts degree program for non-traditional students. This program, which admitted its first students in the spring of 1975, will be making extensive use of learning contracts.

Effects of contract learning on students, faculty,
New College, and the total University of Alabama.

bringing about change in a traditional university

neal r. berte

Art Keeney came to New College of the University of Alabama with a unique problem that needed a unique solution. Art had over thirty years of professional experience in television, radio, and newspaper work, but no college degree. He had edited newspapers, scripted national news broadcasts, and was at the time everything in a public relations capacity for a city school board. He wanted an interdisciplinary depth study in communication-education and an undergraduate degree.

If Art had entered any other division of the university he would have begun with only eight hours credit; however, through New College and with the help of the Departments of Broadcast and Film Communication and Journalism, Art received fifty-nine hours credit for his past experience in broadcasting and print journalism. He produced cassettes, videotapes, newspapers, awards, and letters of recognition and support to prove his competence in the areas covered by the courses. This credit for past experience, coupled with College Level Examination Placement credit, meant that Art began his college work with seventy semester hours instead of eight.

After his admission to New College, Art continued to weave

journalism, broadcasting, and education into an interdisciplinary depth-study. Before graduation he prepared and completed an independent study to produce a public relations campaign for a halfway house for alcoholics. To carry out the project, Art produced a twenty-minute slide presentation with a script that he wrote and taped and over four hundred photographs that he took. He also designed and edited a twelve-page brochure and wrote over fifty radio and television spots for public service use. He completed the study during the three-week interim term and received academic credit.

Presently Art is working on a master's degree in the Administration of Higher Education, after earning his undergraduate degree in two semesters plus a summer on campus.

mary lynn pike

Mary Lynn Pike entered New College as a sophomore with an interest in social work, particularly with youth. By the spring of her junior year, this interest had developed into the beginnings of a program in correctional psychology, which preceded the university program in correctional psychology by almost two years. She included coursework from a variety of divisions across the campus: child and human development from the School of Home Economics; abnormal psychology and statistics from the Psychology Department; criminology from the Sociology Department; and adjudication of social issues from the Business Law Department. This combination of courses for an interdisciplinary depth-study would have been impossible without New College.

In addition to regular university courses, Mary Lynn designed an independent study through New College entitled "The Disadvantaged Child and His Family." During the project she worked both with the chief probation officer at the juvenile court and with a faculty member from the Human Development Department of the university. She set as her goals a better understanding of the court and the children who pass through it. To meet these goals she met regularly with the probation officer and faculty. In addition, she completed several projects at the court, read books and articles relevant to her study, and kept a journal of her experience. For this project, she received three semester hours of credit.

Mary Lynn chose to spend her last semester before graduation in an out-of-class learning project. She designed an experience with the Law Enforcement Academy at the University of Alabama.

The Academy includes six weeks of full-time training for police recruits from across the state of Alabama. The training covers the gamut from theories of criminology to marksmanship. Mary Lynn proposed to attend the Academy just as a rookie and afterwards spend two weeks with the Director of the Academy evaluating the past session and planning for the next one. In addition, she read several books, completed a paper, and was evaluated by a professor from the Correctional Psychology Department. She received nine semester hours credit for her work with the Law Enforcement Academy. Presently she is attending graduate school in correctional psychology at the University of Alabama.

barbara duke

Barbara Duke entered New College because she "wanted to become a person." She was already enrolled in the arts and sciences division of the university, but she felt she might have a more meaningful experience in the New College. Her academic interests were primarily with the humanities and the social sciences.

Barbara eventually put together a depth-study in correctional psychology with a long-range goal of psychology graduate school. (This was eventually modified to an interest in law school.) She completed a number of independent studies and had an unusual off-campus experience for academic credit.

In one independent study, "Original Ideas in Modern Science Fiction," Barbara read a number of science fiction works, extracting original ideas and developing social commentaries. She read over thirty novels in the course of a semester and received three hours of academic credit. In another independent study, she designed a ten-hour-a-week internship with a local law firm. Her activities included doing legal research and investigation and observing court activity. She assisted in the preparation of a brief dealing with Alabama's Sexual Psychopath Statute, which played a research role in the eventual replacement of the law. She received academic credit for this work. In another independent study, she completed a research study on the "Attitudes Toward Women in the Legal System." She developed research, which included designing and validating a research questionnaire and administering the questionnaire to three hundred subjects. She analyzed her results and compared them to associated published papers. For this experience she received three hours credit.

The summer before her graduation, Barbara designed an out-of-class learning experience with the Fulton County Juvenile Court in Atlanta, Georgia. The experience involved working as an assistant probation officer in the Dependency and Neglect Division and as a psychological counselor in the Juvenile Detention Center. The internship was a full-time position and lasted for twelve and one-half weeks. She was assigned her own caseload and did home visits, investigations, and testified in court on behalf of her clients. Barbara received nine semester hours credit for the experience. She has been admitted to law school.

eddie o'neil

Eddie O'Neil transferred to New College as a sophomore. He had previously been an English major but desired a depth-study which would provide a broader orientation to the humanities—particularly English, history, and philosophy. Law school was a definite postgraduate goal, so he also needed an acquaintance with the social sciences.

New College allowed him to fulfill his humanities depth-study, primarily in a traditional mode. He took courses ranging from the American novel and Oriental philosophy to accounting and computer science. In addition to these regular classroom courses, Eddie completed an independent study entitled "Backgrounds to Literature." In the course of a semester he read various works of Freud, Darwin, Marx, and other social, political, and psychological thinkers who had influenced late nineteenth and twentieth century literature. He met with the instructor every other week. They discussed the readings and their influence on modern writers.

During his junior year Eddie worked for two semesters as an administrative intern for the dean of New College. For these two experiences he received six hours of academic credit. In the course of his internship he became interested in developing new out-of-class learning programs for students at the University of Alabama. He, along with two other New College students, decided to develop a Volunteer Service Bureau for the campus, working through the University Year for ACTION (UYA) program. UYA is a federal program administered by both New College and the School of Social Work. It allows students to work full-time off campus on some type of community service project. UYA students receive academic credit and a cost-of-living stipend.

The students' efforts led to not only Volunteer Service Office but also several new internship programs for credit. For his year's experience, Eddie received eighteen hours of academic credit and was able to take a few traditional courses during the year, so that he earned a total of a full year's credit. In an evaluation of the experience, he said that he had gained numerous insights into political science, economics, and administration. He has since been admitted to law school.

opening options for students and faculty

As these four examples indicate, New College at the University of Alabama represents a departure from the traditional approach to the undergraduate educational experience at the university and from most institutions nationally. New College, initiated in 1970, has a two-part mandate: (1) to create an opportunity for a highly individualized approach to undergraduate education utilizing contract-learning, which draws freely from the extensive and diverse scholarship of the entire university faculty and from external learning resources; and (2) to serve the university as an experimental unit with the expectation that program concepts, examination and measurement methods, teaching modes, facilities, and personnel will provide an experimental base for modifications to other components of the university's programs.

As related to the first purpose of the New College, the individualized curricular approach, there are a number of features of this educational experience which should be mentioned: (1) The use of the learning contract for planning purposes; (2) Admission of a cross section of students with varied educational and vocational goals; (3) A concept of advising that deals with the total development of the individual; (4) A problem-focused approach to general education through interdisciplinary seminars; (5) A recommended out-of-class learning experience for academic credit; (6) The use of depth study programs involving both traditional and nontraditional areas of specialization; and (7) Individualized graduation requirements and evaluation procedures.

The New College is an "administrative college," since roughly two-thirds to three-fourths of the students' work is done outside of the College. Through the New College, students are enrolled in courses across the university, representing any of the various colleges in such a way that educational experiences are packaged to meet students' individual needs. They are able to draw on educational experiences from three thousand course offerings available at the University of Alabama. By individualizing the educational program through the New College, the only additional courses offered are a set of interdisciplinary problem-focused seminars and the opportunity for out-of-class learning experiences. Thus there is no need to duplicate faculty and resources already available at the university. Students receive either a Bachelor of Arts or a Bachelor of Science degree, depending upon the area in which they do their depth-study.

The basic assumptions which underlie the above objectives include the following: (1) that each individual is unique with different needs; (2) that an educational program should be developed which reflects the interests and capabilities of each student; (3) that opportunities should be provided for an individual to be able to learn to think and to deal with principles and concepts rather than simply to memorize data; (4) that students are capable of accepting much of the responsibility for their own learning when given the opportunity to do so; (5) that what someone knows is more important than how they gained that knowledge; (6) that significant learning occurs outside of class as well as within; that is, that learning is not bound by time or place; (7) that problem-focused, general education experiences of an interdisciplinary nature which demonstrate the integration of knowledge are highly desirable in our modern-day world; and (8) that part of the role of the faculty member is that of a colearner and a mentor in the learning process as well as a source of assistance in the process of acquiring knowledge.

During the 1970-1971 academic year, twenty students were enrolled in the New College as a pilot project group. The current enrollment is approximately two hundred students. An additional 250 students are enrolled in some of the programs of the New College, even though they are enrolled in other divisions of the university.

Since the New College is not an honors college, the program is available to students from a wide range of academic backgrounds and levels of intellectual achievement, provided they manifest a significant level of motivation and intellectual independence. An attempt is made with the selection procedures to enroll a representative cross-section of students in terms of ability, age, sex, race, and professional, educational, or vocational interests.

The student, with faculty, community or student advisors or both, plans his program of studies in the context of a Contract-

Advising Committee. Usually no more than four individuals serve on this committee, and the only criterion for service is that a particular individual has something definite to contribute to the educational and vocational planning for that particular student. The student's individual needs, desires, capacities, motivations, familial and social influences, as well as his academic performance are taken into consideration by the Contract-Advising Committee, which is mainly concerned about the student's total development. The first question on the learning contract is "What are your educational and vocational goals?" This becomes the circumscribing influence for the planning of each student's program. The student assumes the responsibility for getting the advice from members of the Contract-Advising Committee and for entering the material on the learning contract.

The concept of the contract is used to suggest a mutual responsibility on the part of the student and the New College. Regularly updated with the assistance of the Contract-Advising Committee, the graduation contract provides the framework for the educational development of each student in the New College. It is possible to modify the contract every semester or every year, with the approval of the student's Contract-Advising Committee. Final approval of the depth-study plan by the New College Review Committee should occur within a year of expected graduation if a student has put together a nontraditional area of specialization.

On the contract students can note any credit for advanced placement, performance on proficiency exams, or prior learning experience which has been certified by members of the New College staff. Additional information requested on the contract includes plans for an out-of-class learning experience including proposed type of experience, dates, and location, an opportunity to record the main decisions made and areas discussed in each contract-advising session, plans for courses and educational experiences to be taken in the depth-study area, as well as electives to be added to the student's program. In addition, a checklist attached to each contract worksheet raises a number of questions that the members of the Contract-Advising Committee might want to think about on a fairly regular basis.

New College encourages its students to pursue their academic interests outside of the classroom through independent study and through out-of-class learning experiences for credit. In both cases learning contracts are used and the student must prepare a clear, concise statement including the course area, topic, or problem he intends to study; his reasons for doing the particular study; his tentative plans for background reading, bibliography, and outline; his plans to initiate the study; and the anticipated outcomes of the study. Independent study options are available in conjunction with either approach to depth-study as an additional means by which a student may extend the study of his particular interest. Prior to involvement in independent study, the student must enter into an agreement with a supervising faculty member in such a way that he sets forth his plan for the proposed independent study. Evaluative criteria are established by the student and his instructor prior to the student's receiving a class card for independent study.

testing the effects of new college

All New College students take a standard test battery composed of basic tests administered to all incoming students at the university and a special test battery developed in the New College. This initial testing serves as the baseline against which future testing is compared, so that standardized test data can be used to relate New College student development and changes in the general population. The standardized measures consist of the basic university program for all new students—School and College Abilities Test, and American College Test (initial testing only)—as well as the additional New College battery—the Survey of Study Habits and Attitudes, the Omnibus Personality Inventory, the Allport-Vernon-Lindzey Study of Values, and the Revised Strong Vocational Interest Inventory. Basic information about the location of each student is kept after graduation, and each graduate has been asked to participate in a follow-up study every three years.

Recognizing that many experiences which may have a significant impact on student development are not necessarily structured learning activities, Berte and Upshaw (1971) suggest that Student Life Studies can identify significant factors in education not measured by traditional tests (Berte and Upshaw, 1971). Consequently, a Student Life Studies Program is a part of the evaluation of the New College. This research approach has been utilized by other institutions with some success. Small groups of students (approximately ten) are randomly chosen from the New College so as to represent all of the interdisciplinary seminars. Similar groups representing the various schools and colleges are randomly chosen from the parent university to serve as a comparison group. Through weekly meetings of small groups of students with faculty, community or staff persons including undergraduate and graduate interns serving as leaders, information is gathered about the perceived experiences that students are having and reports are then shared with administrators and faculty as a way to promote greater understanding of the educational experiences available on the campus.

Another evaluation approach is the use of unobtrusive measures. Since New College has a basic mandate to influence the university in the direction of educational innovation and reform, it is necessary to measure some variables that may not be as apparent as others, which show the New College impact on the campus. The following are some examples of indirect measures of possible effects of the New College on the university: (1) write-ups of the New College in on-campus and off-campus publications such as newspapers, magazines, and so on, which New College does not generate on its own; (2) faculty applications to teach in New College; (3) student applications to enroll in New College; (4) requests for catalogs and additional information from students, parents, and others external to New College; (5) transfers from schools in divisions within the university; (6) attrition of students, faculty, and staff from New College; and (7) visits by representatives of other institutions of higher education and requests for information about New College.

In an effort to obtain feedback from nonpartisan individuals, outside consultants visit New College on a fairly regular basis. After reviewing available collected data, observing the educational operations, and meeting with students, staff, and administrators, the team submits an evaluation report which is discussed in the context of staff meetings and retreats.

As to the evaluation of faculty members, they are evaluated twice each semester by their students, at mid-term and at the end of the semester. The instructor is rated on a scale which utilizes a continuum with extremes representing least and most desirable characteristics. The results of the mid-semester evaluation are made available to the instructor in order that he may make adjustments where appropriate and to indicate to him the students' perceptions of the course at that point in time. The final evaluation by students serves as a basis for an end-of-semester conference between the faculty member and the Dean.

In keeping with the contract program and the emphasis on goal development at the New College there is a special assessment instrument for New College faculty and staff known as the growth contract. Each semester all members of the faculty and staff (clerical staff included) formulate a growth contract as a way to make practical an underlying assumption of the New College, namely, that faculty and staff members are in a colearning relationship with students, versus more traditional approaches in which the faculty member becomes the primary source for all learning and enters into no agreement to continue his or her own learning. The concept of growth implies change and the idea of a contract connotes a mutual obligation. The following are four elements included in the growth contract: (1) Specific goals and plans for action as related to the teaching-learning process. This may include experimentation with new techniques, use of new resources, and development of different evaluation approaches. (2) Growth of a professional nature—readings, development of articles and materials for publication, attendance at various meetings, completion of projects may be considered in this category. (3) Making specific commitments to one's obligations as related to the New College in terms of effective undergraduate teaching, advising, and other research and service activities. (4) Matters related to personal growth and development.

Faculty members also evaluate student development in each of their seminars. Faculty members are asked to evaluate the students in three areas during the course of the semester. These areas include the cognitive, skill, and affective areas of development. The student and faculty member in a one-to-one relationship engage in this kind of evaluation activity at the beginning of the semester and the student and faculty member go through this process again at the end of the semester. These evaluations become a part of the material available to the student's contract-advising committee for purposes of evaluation of the student's performance and development of an educational program on a semester-by-semester basis.

During each spring of the academic year, students, faculty and other administrators on the campus have an opportunity to review and evaluate the work of the dean of the New College. This is done principally through an evaluation instrument which is completed anonymously by the various constituencies served. A three page survey instrument provides an opportunity for the individuals representative of the categories noted above to evaluate the dean in terms of his general administrative ability, instructional leadership, professional leadership, and personal development.

After the first year of operation, the staff of the New College requested that the president of the university establish a New College Review Committee. This body is composed of faculty members who represent various colleges across the campus and their role is to review any depth-study program that does not fit into traditional disciplinary structures. This committee represents all colleges of the university and includes students and faculty. The New College Review Committee has been of immeasurable assistance both in formal and informal ways and these individuals have added an element of due process which is an important dimension of the contract-learning process.

conclusion

Five years of experiences and evaluation data provide substantial evidence that most of the students enrolled in this contract learning program are satisfied with their experiences, basically for three reasons: (1) that through the contract-advising process students can turn to competent individuals who care about their educational and vocational future and about them as persons; (2) that they are participating in a new form of learning through the interdisciplinary seminars dealing with contemporary problems; and (3) that if they wish to go on to additional professional or graduate training, they have not been penalized by virtue of participation in this contract-learning program.

In addition, one of the purposes of the New College is to serve the university as an experimental base for modifications to undergraduate education. A number of developments have taken place since the New College has been in existence, for example: (1) evidence of more interdisciplinary attempts among departments and divisions on the campus to cooperate with other divisions and to develop various courses and programs through the New College; (2) the creation of a Special Studies Major option in the College of Arts and Sciences, which enables students to individualize their undergraduate experiences in a much more flexible curriculum; (3) the adoption of the Internship Program in business-government-industry, which was initially established in New College and taken over by the College of Commerce and Business Administration, as well as the offering of other internship programs in other divisions of the university for academic credit; (4) the garnering of federal government and private foundation resources for innovative educational approaches, which have been utilized across the university for the benefit of improving the teaching-learning process; (5) the recognition and encouragement of outstanding teaching as the number one priority for promotion and tenure for some faculty members—a policy adopted early by New College and now accepted by more divisions of the university; (6) the implementation of an External Degree Program for adult learners utilizing learning contracts.

While New College is certainly not without its difficulties, the use of the contract-learning model has facilitated the individualization of the undergraduate educational experience for a number of students and has contributed to some additional options for teaching and learning on the campus of the University of Alabama.

reference

Berte, N. R., and Upshaw, C. "Student Life Studies: An Action Research Option." *National Association of Student Personnel Administrators Journal,* 1971, *9* (1), 77-80.

Reasons why advising is an especially
important responsibility of any
institution engaged in contract programs.

advising for goal development and assessment of educational resources

bernard j. sloan

Learning is one of the most personal of all human endeavors. The basic assumption of contract programs in education, therefore, is the idea that each individual's educational goals should be the primary consideration in designing experiences for significant learning. In developing contracts, then, the programs should not have a procrustean nature. They should embrace the concept of education as a continuing process; they should be forward-looking in development and in evaluation so that students can build future programs out of the needs and experiences derived from previous ones. Programs should seek to enhance affective as well as cognitive forces; they should provide for appropriate skill development. Institutional goals should be designed to include formative evaluation (assessing an ongoing experience in order to have in-progress impact on the experience) as well as summative evaluation (assessing an experience in its entirety, usually at its end).

77

advising

An essential institutional responsibility in a contract learning program of this type is the provision of an appropriate system of student advising through the tutor or mentor relationship as well as by academic counselor and peer counselors.

A function of advising is to facilitate goal development. For our purposes goals can be understood as expectations that may exist at varying levels of the student's awareness. The advisor must first recognize individual differences and perceive advising students as a major professional responsibility. Then he must make the student aware of the available advising services, encourage him to use them, and offer adequate and specific opportunities for the services to take place. Students should be made aware of the available resources such as student services, placement and testing, as well as opportunities for out-of-class learning.

In his interaction with the student, the advisor should lead the student to understand that the principle responsibility for his development rests with himself and not with the institution. This will not always be an easy task, because most students do not know how to cope with such a revolutionary concept. Next the student must be led to perceive a need for goal development. This may be accomplished as simply as asking "What are your educational goals?" The student may not have thought about his future in terms of goal development and may not understand the question thoroughly at first.

Goal development is a process of continuous change with *goal-setting* as only one part of the process. Every learning activity affects goal development by confirming a goal already set or by providing data that lead to goal alteration. Too many advising programs skip from episode to episode of goal-setting and provide little framework or encouragement for students to perceive the goal development process or to capitalize on the self-understanding inherent in this process.

In the typical advising program, student meets a faculty member once or twice a year, perhaps even less, and if the question of goals is discussed at all it usually involves trying to identify a set goal; little attention goes to the larger and continuing process of goal development. In leading a student to develop his or her own goals, the advisor should encourage the student to examine the available information, to seek new information concerning goals, and to consider the vocational implications of the available choices. If a radical departure from a previous goal is involved, students should be encouraged to assess the risk and cost involved in the alternatives, as well as to understand the goal development process which has taken place. Then they should be helped to outline strategies for pursuing the new goals.

The advising process should be devoted to raising the students' consciousness that goal-altering—change and growth—is basic to the human condition. Students should not feel undue anxiety if a lifelong or childhood goal suddenly changes upon exposure to new information.

With this concept of continuous change in mind the student should be led to recognize that the process of change based on his experiences—both academic and nonacademic—should be understood in terms of the future. The question should be asked at every point, "Where has this development led us?"

The idea of continuous change mandates continuous feedback. Such feedback must be facilitated by the ready accessibility of the advisor on an informal basis along with designated or scheduled meetings with the student. One meeting per academic term is barely a satisfactory minimum. Also there should be as much collaboration as possible, with the student playing an important role in goal development. This tends to negate the possibility of any adversary or generation-gap relationship developing (Hodgkinson, 1971). Since advising should emphasize improvement of the student's strengths as well as minimizing his weaknesses, a lowered threat level between the advisor and student should emerge. They should become collaborators working for the student's best interests.

advantages of goal-oriented advising

An individualized advising process which places heavy emphasis on goal development provides several advantages. It offers the student an opportunity to participate actively in the design and implementation of his learning process, according to his individual needs. The individual emphasis in the advising process makes each session likely to hold experiences which the student is ready for and finds challenging. This procedure maximizes the possibility of developing an educational program which relates learning to previously developed interests of the student and may win him to the intellectual enterprise. The student can also develop close personal relationships with faculty members who are willing to assist him in identifying personal capacities and limitations (Ottawa University, 1970).

Another advantage of the individualized advising process is that the student can add greatly to his inventory of learning resources, especially the resources available beyond the classroom. Having a student locate and organize many of his own learning opportunities supports the important concept of shifting responsibility for learning from the institution to the student.

deciding on learning tasks

To select among various options, advisors and students should consider several questions before deciding on a particular learning experience, wherever it is offered. First, "How does the resource relate to the student's educational goals, and is it consistent with the goals of the institution?" This question is especially important if a large amount of student time is to be invested in the resource. It is also important to determine whether the resource leads to other learning experiences and provides for both cognitive and affective learning (that is, whether the experience satisfies the principles of continuity and interaction). Advisor and student should discuss what linkages a particular learning resource can provide with previous scholarship and decide how best the total experience can be evaluated in terms of cognitive and affective growth, skill development, acquisition of theoretical knowledge, and so forth. Both formative and summative evaluation strategies should be planned and included in the contract before the student embarks on a learning experience. The experience will provide the learner with opportunities to examine, exercise, and expand his or her own system of values, thus furthering the overall process of goal development.

To sum up briefly, several principles underlie student goal development and the assessment of educational resources in contract learning programs. First, learning is a personal activity and is best achieved in an institutional setting when the institution fosters learning as a function of individual goal development. Second, the responsibility for learning should rest primarily with the student and not with the institution. Third, evaluation procedures should be an early consideration in any learning experience, and they should be designed to assist the learner in developing future-oriented rather than past-oriented educational goals. The principles of continuity and interaction should be a guide in seeking and assessing learning experiences. Fourth, goal development is an open-ended, continuing process—mere goal-setting is not enough. Fifth, traditional models of advising should be improved on or replaced, to facilitate goal development.

The contract model is an excellent organizational device to facilitate the implementation of these principles. In any decision-making process, the clearer one's goals, the easier his decisions become, and contract programs, along with their concomitant advising procedures, maximize this principle of individual goal development.

references

Hodgkinson, H. L. "Assessment and Reward Systems." In G. K. Smith (Ed.), *New Teaching, New Learning*. San Francisco: Jossey-Bass, 1971.
Ottawa University Self Study Committee. *The New Plan of Education for Ottawa University*. (2nd ed.) Ottawa, Kansas: Ottawa University, 1970.

Bernard J. Sloan is associate dean of the New College at The University of Alabama, project director for its External Degree Program, and coordinator of Out-of-Class Learning. He has been involved in innovative educational programs elsewhere in Alabama and other states, including voluntary consortia and educational television, as well as in working directly with students in a teaching-advising capacity.

*Individualized learning requires individualized
evaluation as well as teaching, and
needs its own assessment of success in
accomplishing institutional goals.*

evaluating individualized learning

harold l. hodgkinson

When one thinks about college-level evaluation, one typically thinks of a procedure whereby we rank one student's score on a standardized measure against the other students whose scores form the norm for that measure. Although norm-referenced procedures can still be used in evaluating individualized programs, they are often inappropriate, and their domination of the process has been reduced.

Individualized learning requires individualized processes of evaluation. The more learning is individualized, the more the student needs diagnostic information to perform midcourse correction maneuvers which will make it possible for him to improve on a continuous basis, using feedback from the evaluative process as he goes. Thus, evaluation becomes partially a way of improving, not just measuring, learning. We do want to know whether or not the student attains the goals that were decided; the acquisition of preconceived goals is only one measure of performance and leaves out other unintended components of student learning which may be equally useful.

Individualized learning means working individual student differences into the learning process rather than ignoring them. Evaluation, in order to be consistent, should be flexible, at least partially diagnostic, and centered on the goals of the individual learner. As the learner improves, more of the evaluation process should be in his or her hands through *self*-evaluation.

This problem of evaluation of individualized learning is becoming increasingly more important, due mainly to the trend in many, if not most, institutions to consider granting credit for prior life experiences as well as present off-campus experiences such as field experience and foreign study. Many campuses have resorted to a cut-off score on an instrument such as CLEP, but when one looks at the arbitrary fashion in which these institutional cut-off points are established, the process seems less than equitable. The crediting of all out-of-class learning should be based as much as possible on the circumstances of the individual learner. A variety of evaluative devices will allow the development of a triangulation of where the student actually is, using a variety of standardized tests, self-anchoring scales, simulations, reports from supervisors, logs, diaries, teachers' reports, use of prior learning in new settings, and so on. Such a triangulation procedure, although sometimes more costly, should result in more accurate credit-giving than through any one instrument.

An additional force leading to a focus on evaluation comes from the new interest in accountability and consumerism in higher education: Is the student actually getting what he or she paid for? States are asking the cost-effectiveness questions of institutions: What is the yield, or return, on a dollar of scarce state capital invested in higher education compared to other services designed to improve the quality of life? The first attempts at outcome measurements (credit hours generated per FTE faculty, degrees awarded per FTE faculty, and so on) were at best only proxy measures of student learning. Increased interest is now being shown in developing some measures of educational "value added." How far has each individual student moved from his or her point of entry?

The essence of individualized programs is that the student participates in the formation of the learning activity; it is to some degree self-initiated and self-directed. A student working by himself or herself is not necessarily engaged in an individualized program if what he or she is doing has been entirely predetermined by someone else. For example, a language lab is not necessarily an individualized program of instruction, and neither is the audiotutorial, as the notion is commonly used. These devices are active response producers. They are usually better than having the student in a passive mode, but active responses to another's directions are not enough. Individualized programs require that the learner decides to enter into and partially to structure the activity. Although the evidence is not yet in, I tend to support the view that self-initiated work will produce greater gains in measured student acquisition and retention of knowledge than work initiated by an institution or faculty member.

The same problem applies to the term *independent study*. A student studying all by himself is not necessarily engaged in independent study, unless he has decided what and when study takes place, using advice and consultation. This means that a student who voluntarily decides to take introduction to biology as a large survey course, and is allowed by the instructor to structure the course to meet his or her needs via the Keller Plan, may be engaged in an independent activity which could qualify as independent study. Another student who is sitting by himself reading through the teacher's outline and reading list for a particular course is simply taking that course on a one-student basis. I dwell on this point because we usually think that the term *individualized program* is simply a single student working alone. But one on one is not enough— you can have an individualized learning program with ten or fifteen students in a group all doing pretty much the same thing and in a collaborative way, as long as each student has the right of decision. The focus needs to be on the student's *decision to want to learn, what to learn, and how to learn it.*

Research has taught us very little about the decision to want to learn. (We also know almost nothing about how people forget.) Nonetheless, wanting to learn is at the heart of individualized instruction. It does not mean complete carte blanche to the student, as he or she should be asked to defend choices to a skilled and competent mentor or advisor. The decision should basically be the student's, which is then ratified or reviewed by the faculty.

One major problem in the evaluation of all types of learning is that the measuring device is usually tacked onto the end of the learning sequence, as the final exam is in most courses. Building evaluation strategies right into the learning process seems more useful for checking student progress and diagnosing learning difficulties, in order to maximize the student's level of mastery. Indeed, in many forms, the evaluation process can become one of the most important learning outcomes for the student as he or she moves toward greater self-understanding through a well-designed evaluation strategy. This is certainly the case in contract learning, in good modularization, in field experience programs, and in many competency-based curricula. This view, that evaluation (for the improvement of student learning) is a continuous, integral part of the teaching and learning strategy, is in marked contrast to the traditional view that only the final, or summative, evaluation is of any importance. Even if a student does well on a final exam, the norm-referenced A is of no use in helping the student improve. Some students say that getting an unexplained A is more frustrating than getting an unexplained C or D. Certain end-point evaluations are necessary for credentialing and other purposes, but they often interfere with teaching and advising functions.

For this reason, it is increasingly important that we separate out the functions of advising (basically diagnosis), teaching (basically communication), and credentialing (basically norm-referenced evaluation to see if a person meets some external, often job-related, norm). Many individualized learning programs may not have any credentialing components as such. And many individualized learning programs can proceed without a great deal of formal teaching.

evaluation instruments

A number of instruments are available which will give both an aggregate and individual score on a number of dimensions of personal functioning. Instruments like the Omnibus Personality Inventory, the Allport-Vernon-Lindzey, the Institutional Functioning Inventory, the Experience of College Questionnaire, and the Pace-HEMEK can be used both to develop norms on groups of students and as a pretest-posttest measure of individual student change through time. Unfortunately, none of these instruments has yet been developed to indicate the normal, or expected, changes in student scores through the freshman-senior time period. Only Alexander Astin's work with the American Council on Education-UCLA Cooperative Institutional Research Program data bank can yield expected scores on the measured variables for seniors, based on scores of entering freshmen at that institution. But if faculty members have been trained to use it properly, an instrument like the Omnibus Personality Inventory can be of great diagnostic use in programs of individualized instruction. (Without adequate training,

however, introduction of testing results into the advising and diagnosing arena can be a disaster for the student.) (See also Hodgkinson and others, 1974.)

In many field experience programs, some very good self-rat-
ing scales have been developed, providing for highly individualized
responses as well as a common framework for their interpretation.
Many of the University Year for Action programs are also producing very rigorous yet individualized evaluation instruments for measuring the amount of student change stimulated by the field experience. As one example of what might be learned in this area, Edward
Angus from Mars Hill College, long a leader in field experience education, has reported that students decline markedly on measures of
authoritarianism after the field experience. Before they go out, they
are fairly sure that there are only two kinds of people, good and
bad, and so on. After the field experience, which puts many of
these students into a brand new environment for the first time, they
begin to integrate into their own world view the complexities and
ambiguities that comprise the field situation, moving from a stage
of absolute certainty to relativistic concerns.

One of the most useful procedures for the evaluation of individualized programs is the learning contract. In this form, the student and his advisor agree in advance on the nature of the learning
to be done, the way in which this learning fits into the student's
larger objectives, and the determination of student fulfillment of his
goals. Both the faculty member and student sign the contract,
which then becomes the evaluation base. Learning contracts do
separate advising, teaching, and credentialing functions, although if
the contract is well drawn, the evaluation and diagnostic processes
will be continuous, as well as final. The contract should have within
it formative and summative dimensions of evaluation, both to improve performance and to ascertain whether or not stated goals
have been achieved.

I do not like the idea of having students choose between
learning contract models of different levels of difficulty—an *A* contract for those who wish to work hard, a *B* contract for those who
do not wish to work quite so hard, and so on. A contract should be
a unique and indigenous thing, not subject to comparative judgments. For certain kinds of individualized programs, however,
grades may be useful. As Peter Elbow has said in the *Journal of
Higher Education,* what grades really measure is the affective quality of the teacher's response to student learning. *A*'s and *F*'s are

significant in that they indicate genuine pleasure or genuine pain as the instructor's perception of the student's work. *B*'s and *D*'s indicate the same thing to a lesser degree, while a *C* means that the instructor had no affective response to the student's performance.

It seems to me much better, both in learning contracts and in competency-based learning programs generally, to develop criteria in a checklist form and get the checklist to the student early enough to be useful. It can be used a number of times, and, if the student wishes, he can use it as a time-line chart, something like those used in hospitals to chart patients' progress. It can be a multidimensional time-line indicating five or six areas of the student's growth as they relate to the contract or other individualized form of learning agreement. Most important is the elimination of a dominating one-dimensional model of evaluation for individualized programs. For example, knowledge of communication skills may move along a continuum to the point where the student demonstrates verbal and written communication ability through a series of exercises designed to first illustrate knowledge of communication approaches, then comprehension of those theories, followed by evidence of the student's ability to synthesize the knowledge by application to new subject matter areas.

Any criterion for evaluating student progress, like grades, checklists, and so on, should begin to wither away as the student spends more time in the institution, leaving the senior with well-developed abilities to accurately assess his or her own performance without these external aids. Indeed, there should be a major difference between the freshman and the senior, in that the senior should have developed effective ways of analyzing his performance and of knowing when goals have actually been attained.

faculty evaluative skills

Many faculty members do not have the skills to do good evaluative work with students in individualized learning programs. Very little in the typical faculty member's experience has trained him in this area. Empire State, Ottawa, Eckerd, and Minnesota Metro, among others, have discovered that good mentors need different kinds of skills than the typical faculty member possesses.

Particularly in contract learning, the faculty member is often the principal initiator of the evaluation design for that particular student's work. This makes it imperative that faculty members develop a variety of flexible evaluation tools. A less effective alternative is a staff member with evaluative skills to review all contracts and make sure that evaluation designs are feasible and legitimate.

Another problem which faculty members need assistance on is the possibility (and even necessity) that students change goals through time. The contract and the evaluation design within it should be susceptible to the addition of midcourse correction maneuvers, whereby the evaluation design can be modified as the student moves through the program. Thus the final evaluation model will show a more accurate picture of what the student wants to attain.

One of the major needs that emerge for faculty in this kind of program is to develop increasingly sophisticated evaluation models and a broad spectrum of possible evaluation designs for faculty members who work with individualized programs. Graduate schools especially need this, as they turn out increasing numbers of new Ph.D.'s who presumably should have these skills and yet in reality do not. In addition, in-service programs to help develop these skills in existing faculty are also very important.

implications for faculty roles

An emphasis on increased individualization of learner outcomes leads naturally to increased concern with the development of individualized notions of teacher competence. Individualized learning leads directly to notions of individualized teaching, encouraging each teacher to develop the learning-producing skills which most interest him. Certain teachers may wish to focus on skills in advising or seminar teaching, while others may wish to increase their competence in module writing, working in teaching teams, and so on. From this notion, the next logical outgrowth is the idea of differentiated staffing—different teachers can do different things in order to reach a full-time load, rather than figuring faculty load strictly on the number of courses taught. Differentiated staffing assumes, however, that the institution is willing to *pay for* educationally related services, such as advising, committee service, supervising independent study, producing plays and art exhibits, and other highly individualistic skills, by including them in calculations of faculty load.

Individualized learning programs may begin to force the issue of defining what a faculty member's professional areas of skill should be. He must be held accountable for the areas in which he is supposed to be professionally competent, and the institutions that train college teachers (or educate them) will have to be held accountable for inculcating these skills in the teacher-to-be.

In the long run, the movement toward individualized instruction may be very helpful in developing competent faculty members who see teaching pluralistically, as a total number of activities engaged in a variety of settings, which produce student learning. The focus should shift from good teaching to good learning, some of which requires no teaching at all.

campus effects

A final issue involves the impact of individualized learning programs on a college campus, what they mean to the life of the college. What can be reasonably expected in a college which goes heavily into a program of individualized learning, especially through contract models? Here are nine possible results:

(1) Shifts in library usage, both in terms of hours of the day and types of materials used. (A broader spectrum of materials in circulation rather than a heavy concentration on a small number of reserve books.)

(2) Different patterns of student life in the residence and dining areas.

(3) Different patterns of student traffic flow on and off the campus.

(4) Some shifts in faculty load calculation and faculty feelings of where their professional interests center.

(5) Massive complaints from the registrar that things are getting out of hand.

(6) Increasing informal student-faculty interaction over meals in the residence halls, and so forth.

(7) Strong feelings of students' involvement with their education, expressed through questionnaire inventories, changes in personal behavior, and increased production of student self-initiated work.

(8) Increasing criticism of the evaluation structure in conventional classroom settings, as a result of the students' developing of their own evaluation designs for learning contracts.

(9) Some shifts in the attrition rates and in the number of students who take some time off before graduating. (One would anticipate a larger number of students taking some time off, but in addition the

possibility of a larger percentage of the entering class graduating at some time in the future.)

In sum, not only will institutions need to assess individualized programs in new ways, but in addition, with individualization most faculty members will have to subject their own skills and techniques in evaluation to the same rigor they have insisted upon in their students.

references

Hodgkinson, H. L. "Bard Students Correct Themes on Tape." *College and University Bulletin*, March 1968, *20* (10), 2-3.
Hodgkinson, H. L., and others. *A Manual for the Evaluation of Innovative Programs and Practices in Higher Education*. Berkeley: Center for Research and Development in Higher Education, University of California, 1974.

Harold L. Hodgkinson, project director at the Center for Research and Development in Higher Education, University of California, Berkeley, has been active in experimental ventures in higher education since assuming the directorship of the school of education of Simmons College in 1958 and then the deanship of Bard College in 1962. The immediate past president of the American Association for Higher Education, he is increasingly interested in issues of adult personality development, as illustrated by his most recent article, "Adult Development: Implications for Faculty and Administrators," The Educational Record, *Fall 1974, 55 (4), 263-274.*

Basic elements of learning contract systems
and their advantages and disadvantages
as alternative modes of education.

the future for learning contracts

neal r. berte

The preceding case studies of present-day approaches to learning contracts show that contracting implements many of the concepts usually included in any definition of nontraditional study—that learning is not bound by time or place, that what students know is more important than how they have gained that knowledge, that new clientele should be served by higher education, that each student should be treated as an individual with distinctive educational and vocational needs, that faculty and staff members should serve as mentors and learning facilitators for students, that curricula should move away from the pattern of separate and isolated disciplinary offerings to interdisciplinary approaches, and that degrees should be awarded on the basis of competence rather than on the accumulation of a magic number of credits (see also Mayville, 1973, p. 1).

Despite the diversity of approaches within learning contract plans, several basic elements characterize them. First, contract learning requires a clear statement of learning objectives. Such goal-setting is not typically a part of the training of either students or faculty mentors. Contract learning requires not only a willingness on the part of faculty members to ask students, "What are your educational and vocational goals?", but also an ability to assist students with the development of objectives that can be translated into meaningful learning activities appropriate for the student, the faculty member, and the institution which is certifying the educational quality of the activities.

Second, learning contracts are not immutable. In any setting they should have the capacity for change and should be modified according to appropriate shifts in educational or vocational goals. While total lack of structure and complete fluidity is not desirable, flexibility based on considered change in a student's plans and goals should be the hallmark of viable learning contract programs.

Third, the student and mentor should agree on a statement of methodology, approach, and evaluation before any contract is implemented. This statement should describe in as much detail as possible the way the contract will be fulfilled, including appropriate readings, writing, or other creative and work activities, the amount of time to be spent in these endeavors, and the techniques of assessment to be employed in their evaluation. This mutually negotiated and agreed-upon statement is the defining characteristic of contract learning plans, distinguishing them from more common forms of individualized education such as tutorial and independent study.

Fourth, contract learning should be characterized by due process. Either one responsible individual or a group of individuals with competence to supervise and evaluate the experience should participate in the experience from the beginning. Outside examiners, a review committee composed of persons not directly involved in the contract program, and an appeal body should be available in case disagreement arises between student and mentor over fulfillment of the terms of the contract. While the existence of a review committee may create additional problems of articulation and interpretation for the contract learning program, it can allay the anxiety over contracts that many faculty members experience in particularly traditional institutions.

Fifth, systematic evaluation should be characteristic of any contract learning program. As Hodgkinson points out in a preceding article, a midcourse correction may occasionally be necessary in the evaluation approach taken, but periodic and final evaluations are essential to determine the credits to be granted for the learning experience. Some institutions, such as the University Without Walls unit at Morgan State College, specify written evaluations by both the student and the faculty mentor. Others may employ oral examinations or multiple assessments of the product of the experience—a formal paper, a work of art, a photographic essay, a computer program, an oral presentation, or any other evidence. In all cases, evaluation is not only one of the most vital components of the learning contract approach in terms of successful experiences and growth for the student, but it is one of the most essential in establishing the credibility of the program and the credibility of student learning for those who must review the program for approval and support, and for others, such as employers or graduate school admissions committees, who review students' experiences for credentialing or certification.

Finally and most important, a successful contract learning program requires a new role for faculty members—one different from that of the lecturer or instructor who conveys information to students or that of the faculty advisor who merely approves student course choices and tells the student what he can and cannot take. This new role has been symbolized by such new descriptions as *mentor* and *learning facilitator*: it is that of the diagnostician who assists the student with the development and clarification of learning goals, self-understanding, and self-direction. This role stems from the principle that we teach not necessarily by precept but by example in situations—as in contract learning programs—where the interaction between the student and faculty member is great. Among the qualifications for a mentor are these specified by Hartwick College in New York State for its faculty: (1) Know the course requirements. (2) Know the student's college goals. (3) Know the student's career goals. (4) Help the student design ways to apply his goals. (5) Share a common interest, a class or major. (6) Be familiar with offerings in other fields. (7) Be well aware of college resources (Maxwell, 1972, p. 1). In addition, if the contract program aims not merely at learning subject matter in specialized areas but also at the total development of the student as a person—socially, emotionally, and physically, as well as intellectually, the role of the mentor as a diagnostician must include awareness of these other growth needs.

For institutions considering one or another approach to contract learning, it may be well to itemize the advantages or strengths of present programs which manifest the above characteristics and then list the disadvantages or weaknesses of learning contracts.

advantages

In *Education and Identity,* Chickering identified several educational conditions of colleges which can positively or negatively influence student development, such as the development of identity, the development of purpose, and the development of a sense of competence in interpersonal relationships. His evidence suggests that such growth is not fostered "when few electives are offered, when books and print are the sole object of study, when teaching is by lecture, when evaluation is frequent and competitive" (1971, p. 148). Instead, these qualities are developed when students are offered choice, diversity, interaction, and responsibility. As with other forms of individualized programs, learning contracts offer these conditions to students. In traditional learning settings, structures are established which it is felt will produce the learning situation desired. With individualized approaches such as learning contracts, rather than making these structures or constraints the emphasis at the outset, an effort is made to respond to the fact of individual differences and to tailor-make a learning situation by adding structure only as it *supports* learning.

In contrast to more traditional forms of individualized study, contract learning reduces ambiguity for the student in the learning process, because it requires specific learning goals, methodology, and evaluation techniques at the outset of the contract. Moreover, the work involved in the student's development of the contract and in negotiating its provisions with the mentor can be a significant learning experience in and of itself.

Also, the role of faculty and staff members is modified in such a way that they are no longer the source of all truth and wisdom or the authority in the learning process when contracts are used successfully. The contract learning process requires student and faculty dialogue, which unfortunately does not take place with great regularity in many higher education settings.

Finally, the contract model prepares people to live in a "future-oriented" society. The increasing importance of choice and availability of many alternatives and options raises the need for persons in the educational process to develop an ability to deal with principles and concepts, to make educated choices, and to be actively involved in the teaching and learning process. Contract learning certainly encourages this kind of involvement.

A number of weaknesses or disadvantages need to be considered, however, if a complete picture of contract learning is to be provided. First, a number of students feel a kind of undue pressure, which heightens the anxiety level during the learning process. Such students may feel insecure and seek relief through performance in a competitive manner, which may take away from the questioning, experimenting, and probing approach requisite for significant learning to occur.

Second, students are sometimes given the responsibility but little power or authority in determining the bounds of the learning experience or its certification to the satisfaction of the faculty member or mentor. In these cases, there may be a misguided attempt to produce independence through paternalism—a dilemma that many of us have faced in child-rearing.

Third, Feeney and Riley point out in their earlier article that contract learning has not brought the educational "drama" that some had predicted. If, as they note, contract learning is merely an open-ended registration form which is given substance by the collection of course offerings and other resources made available by the college, it may not impose any new models or develop problem-solving skills.

Fourth, this problem is exacerbated by the background of most college faculty members, who come out of traditional graduate training programs and thus have been trained in disciplinary values and faculty priorities that tend to promote a highly conservative and structured learning situation with the educational contract. Contract learning programs require a broader range of faculty competence, not necessarily in terms of the knowledge areas but in terms of the ability to work well with students as an advisor or mentor as well as supervisor of the learning experience.

Fifth, a number of the authors in this volume have pointed out that contract learning demands strong motivation by the student. Some students are more inclined than others to take advantage of this kind of added involvement in the learning process, and while contracts allow for increased creativity, they do not insure or create creativity.

A sixth disadvantage of the contract system is that, if taken seriously, its goal of individualization throws the college degree "up for grabs" in terms of experience needed, time taken, and such issues as "How do I know when I am through?" The learning contract as the vehicle for individualization seems to be one strategy for flexibility that permits and requires regular questions but does not necessarily give answers on how each individual student is to pursue his or her educational and vocational goals.

A number of additional factors need to be considered. In an era of already limited financial resources, the cost of contract learning programs is critical. Although its development may have minimal costs, as pointed out by Feeney and Riley, the long-range expense of an individualized curricular approach may cost much more than traditional curricula, particularly as one contemplates the need for additional training of faculty and staff members. If institutions have a contract learning program located within a larger institutional setting, then it is possible to run the contract learning program inexpensively (such as that illustrated by the University Without Walls unit at Morgan State). Another point (illustrated by New College at the University of Alabama) is that contract learning programs can generate additional resources from private foundations and federal government sources; these monies could be utilized across a large university to promote nontraditional approaches to teaching and learning, beyond just the contract learning program. Yet the question remains as to how this kind of individualization can be maximized and yet retain the economies of scale of institutions. The need to make this kind of individualization economically viable becomes even more critical for the future. Yet in an era of varied marketing approaches to entice students into higher education, this particular innovative approach does not necessarily enhance the "marketability" of an institution, as witnessed by the recent financial exigency at New College, Sarasota.

conclusion

Even though learning contracts may take extra time, in an era of dwindling enrollments institutions may do better to use the time for contract learning programs with individual students than to spend time and money gearing up for the next major increase in enrollment or a new building program.

Additional research data is needed to indicate more clearly what happens to students who go through contract learning programs. Chickering presents survey data indicating student satisfaction with the contract learning process; information is also needed on the effectiveness of this approach in meeting stated objectives as compared to other teaching and learning methods.

The need seems imperative to plan a program of longitudinal follow-up studies of evaluation the effects of learning contracts in any setting. At a time when the accountability issues loom large in society, it no longer suffices to say that "intuitively we think that what we are doing here is right" (see Hodgkinson, 1974, p. 82).

More attention must also be given to the fact that contract learning necessitates special training opportunities for faculty and staff members. Retooling faculty and staff to teach differently in a contract learning program has the goal of helping faculty learn how to supervise learning rather than to dispense it. Shifting the center from teaching as such to student-centered learning so that the faculty member is viewed as a colearner is essential.

Finally, there is some indication that faculty members are interested in working in these kinds of programs are more committed to undergraduate teaching and advising than to research and publication. This may necessitate the development of a reward system that encourages recognition for the successful performance of the facilitative role of mentor or advisor, versus the more traditional emphasis on research and publication.

In summary, the evidence is certainly not all in regarding the effectiveness of individualization approaches and more particularly the use of the contract learning model. But many institutions are implementing contract learning programs with the hope of including them with an academic reform movement in higher education that will enhance the opportunities for each student to find the best set of learning experiences to help him create a full and satisfying life. The history of American higher education is replete with examples of earlier approaches to individualization of the undergraduate experience. President Eliot's elective system at Harvard, multiple tracking and ability grouping, student-designed majors, student-designed courses, directed readings, independent study, tutorials, and alternative paths to meeting specific competency requirements are some of the approaches which contrast with the Lancastrian system of mass producing students through a totally prescribed and regimented sequential curriculum.

I am not advocating contract learning as a panacea for higher education nor an all-out "student right or wrong" movement. Appropriate limits have to be carefully determined for what represents viable learning experiences within the various approaches to contract learning. Compared to past generations, students entering college today differ widely in their abilities, their high school experiences, their goals, their demographic characteristics; and the demand is likely to increase for a wider spectrum of educational activity from which students at all levels may choose. The recommendations emerging from the various commission reports which have appeared in the last decade all argue for more variety in college programs, for more alternatives in curricula and for a greater emphasis in meeting the needs of the individual student rather than prepackaging educational experiences with the assumption that these experiences are right for all. The use of the contract learning approach offers a viable option to achieve these goals.

references

Chickering, A. W. *Education and Identity*. San Francisco: Jossey-Bass, 1969.

Hodgkinson, H. L. and others. *A Manual for the Evaluation of Innovative Programs and Practices in Higher Education*. Berkeley, Calif.: Center for Research and Development in Higher Education, 1974.

Maxwell, H. B. *Evidences of Change in the Individual Student*. Proposal to Committee for Institutional Research. Hartwick College, December 1972.

Mayville, W. "Contract Learning." *Research Currents*, ERIC Clearinghouse on Higher Education, December 1973, p. 1.

Accountability, evaluation related to, 84, 99

Administration, increased costs of, in contract system, 29

Admissions: in contract system, 25, 26-27; document of prior learning for, 42-43; to UWW/Morgan State, 42

Adults, as students, 3, 42

Advising: for deciding on learning tasks, 80; for goal development, 77-81; goal-oriented, advantages of, 79-80

Alabama, University of, New College at, vii, 7, 65-76, 98

Allport-Vernon-Lindzey Study of Values, 72, 86

American College Test, 72

American Council on Education-UCLA Cooperative Institutional Research Program, 86

Angus, E., 87

Applied contract, 22

Assessment, of learning experiences under contract system, 34, 39-40, 47, 49

Astin, A. W., 86

Attrition, in contract system, 25, 27

Authority, higher education related to, 9-10

Barnes, E. H., vii

Baskin, S., 51

Berte, N. R., vii-viii, 1-7, 65-76, 93-100

Bloom, B. S., 33, 40

Bradley, P., 31n

Carnegie Commission on Higher Education, 2

Cheek, K. V., 41-42, 51

Chickering, A. W., 31-40, 96, 98-99

College Level Examination Program, 4, 65, 84

Commission on Non-Traditional Study, 2, 7

Competency, as basis for UWW contracts, 42

Contracting for grades, 1

Contracts, learning: advising for, 77-81; applied, 22; assessment of, 34, 39-40; authority related to, 10; benefits of, 4-6, 27, 28, 96; concepts underlying, 2-3, 77; costs of, 28-29, 49-51, 98; defined, vii, 2, 54; elements of, 2, 54, 93-95; as evaluation procedure, 87; examples of, 17-23, 35-38, 43-49, 56-60, 61-62, 65-69; exclusive use of, 7; explanation of, 12-15; faculty role in, 5, 89-90, 95, 96, 97, 99; future of, 93-100; growth of, 6-7; individualization related to, 1-7; for intellectual competence, 31-40; as learning process, 4-5; limits of, 25-27, 39, 97-98; methodological, 18; as nontraditional study, 93; off-campus study, 23; options created by, 69-72; out-of-class, 53-63; practical considerations in adopting, 27-29; process of, 42-49, 70-72; research, 20; self-inquiry about, 32-33; skill, 21; survey, 17; thematic, 19; types of, 16-25

Costs: administrative, 29; advising, 49; contracting, 49-51; of establishing contract system, 28-29; long-range, 98

Craig, A. S., 41-52

Credit by examination, as individualized learning, 4, 65

Credit for experience, as individualized learning, 4, 65, 84

Cross-cultural learning, field study as, 54-59

Curriculum, in contract system, 16, 24

Dash, E., 1, 7

Debus, D., 31n

Dougherty, D., 16n

Dressel, P. L., 4-5, 7

Duke, B., 67-68

Elbow, P., 87
Eliot, C. W., 3, 99
Empire State College, vii, 88; contract system at, 7, 31-40
Evaluation: criteria for, 84; formative and summative, 77, 87; importance of, 84; of individualized learning, 83-91; instruments for, 86-88
Experience of College Questionnaire, 86
External degree programs, as individualized learning, 3-4

Faculty: evaluation by, 88-89; evaluation of, 73-74; growth contracting by, 1, 74; options for, 69-72; qualifications for, 95; quality of, 26; rewards for, 99; role of, 5, 89-90, 95, 96, 97, 99; and students, interaction of, 24-25, 26
Feeney, J., 9-30, 97, 98
Field education: authoritarianism reduced by, 87; defined, 53; elements of, 59; examples of, 61-62; as out-of-class contract within a discipline, 59
Field study: criteria for, 55; defined, 53; examples of, 56-59; as out-of-class contracting, 54-59

General education, example of contract for, 44-45
Goal development: advising for, 77-81; principles of, 80-81; process of, 78-79
Goals, defined, 78
Grades: contracting for, 1; in individualized programs, 87-88
Group projects, field education as, 61-62
Growth contracting: defined, 1; elements of, 74; at New College, Alabama, 74

Hartwick College, 95
Harvard University, elective plan at, 3, 99
Higher education: authority related to, 9-10; egalitarianism of, 3; for self-education, 3

Hodgkinson, H. L., vii, 79, 81, 83-91, 94, 99, 100
Hook, S., 25, 29

Independent study: defined, 53; effectiveness of, 60-61; elements of, 59; examples of, 59-60; as out-of-class contract within a discipline, 59, 71; self-initiation of, 85
Individualization: contracting related to, 1-7; evaluating, 83-91; features of, 69-70; grades in, 87-88; history of, 2-3; self-initiation in, 84-85; urgency for, 3-4
Institutional Functioning Inventory, 86
Institutions, effect of contract learning on, 65-76, 90-91
Intellectual competence: contracts for, examples of, 33-38; development of, 31-40; skills in, 33
Internship, example of contract for, 43, 46-49

Justin Morrill College, vii, 53-63

Keeney, A., 65-66
Keller Plan, 85

Lehmann, T., 31n
Lifelong learning, out-of-class contract learning related to, 63
Lill, L., 31n
Lipsett, L., 31n

McCormick, J., 31n
Mars Hill College, 87
Maxwell, H. B., 95, 100
Mayville, W., 93, 100
Methodological contract, 18
Michigan State University, Justin Morrill College at, vii, 7, 53-63
Minnesota Metropolitan College, 88
Minority persons, as UWW students, 42
Morgan State College, UWW at, vii, 7, 41-52, 94-95, 98

New College (Sarasota), vii, 98; contracts at, experience with, 7, 9-30
New College (University of Alabama),

vii, 65-76, 98; effects of, tested, 72-75; purposes of, 69

Newman Taskforce, 2

New York, State University of, Empire State College of, 31-40

Off-campus study contract, 23

Omnibus Personality Inventory, 72, 86

O'Neil, E., vii, 68-69

Ottawa University, 80, 81, 88

Out-of-class contracts: experience with, at Justin Morrill, 53-63; life-long learning related to, 63; process for, at New College, Alabama, 71-72

Pace-HEMEK, 86

Palola, E., 31n

Pike, M. L., 66-67

Plato, 5

Prisoners, as UWW students, 42

Research contract, 20

Riley, G., 9-30, 97, 98

Rosel, N., 16n

School and College Abilities Test, 72

Skill contract, 21

Sloan, B. J., vii, 77-81

Socrates, 5

South Florida, University of, New College merger with, 11

Strong Vocational Interest Inventory, Revised, 72

Student Life Studies Program, at New College, Alabama, 72-73

Students: adult, 3, 42; attention to, 4; contracts rated by, 34, 39-40, 47, 49, 75, 98-99; development of, 72-73, 74, 96; and faculty, interaction of, 24-25, 26; initiative and responsibility of, 4-5, 84-85; maturity of increased, 4; options for, 69-72; responsibility of, in contract system, 11, 54, 71, 78, 97; self-assessment by, 88; types of, at UWW/Morgan State, 42

SUNY, Empire State College of, 31-40

Survey contract, 17

Survey of Study Habits and Attitudes, 72

Teaching, techniques unchanged in contract system, 24

Thematic contract, 19

Tomas, J., 31n

Union for Experimenting Colleges and Universities (UECU), 41, 51

University Without Walls (UWW), at Morgan State College, vii, 41-52, 94-95, 98

University Year for Action (UYA), 68, 87

Unobtrusive measures, in use at New College, Alabama, 73

Upshaw, C., 72, 76

Veterans, as UWW students, 42

Waterman, A., 25, 29

Women, as UWW students, 42

NEW DIRECTIONS QUARTERLY SOURCEBOOKS

New Directions for Higher Education is one of three quarterly publications of Jossey-Bass Inc., Publishers. Each series provides concise, practical, and timely assistance on a pressing educational topic. Topics and issue editors for each series are listed below.

Yearly subscription rates for each series are $25 for institutions, libraries, and agencies, and $15 for individuals when paid by personal check. To subscribe, or to receive further information, write: *New Directions* Subscriptions, Jossey-Bass Inc., Publishers, 615 Montgomery Street, San Francisco, California 94111.

NEW DIRECTIONS FOR HIGHER EDUCATION
JB Lon Hefferlin, Editor-in-Chief
1973—1. *Facilitating Faculty Development,* Mervin Freedman
2. *Strategies for Budgeting,* George Kaludis
3. *Services for Students,* Joseph Katz
4. *Evaluating Learning and Teaching,* Robert Pace
1974—5. *Encountering the Unionized University,* Jack Schuster
6. *Implementing Field Experience Education,* John Duley
7. *Avoiding Conflict in Faculty Personnel Practices,* Richard Peairs
8. *Improving Statewide Planning,* James Wattenbarger, Louis Bender
1975—9. *Planning the Future of the Undergraduate College,* Donald Trites
10. *Individualizing Education by Learning Contracts,* Neal Berte

NEW DIRECTIONS FOR COMMUNITY COLLEGES
Arthur M. Cohen, Editor-in-Chief
Florence B. Brawer, Associate Editor
1973—1. *Toward a Professional Faculty,* Arthur Cohen
2. *Meeting the Financial Crisis,* John Lombardi
3. *Understanding Diverse Students,* Dorothy Knoell
4. *Updating Occupational Education,* Norman Harris
1974—5. *Implementing Innovative Instruction,* Roger Garrison
6. *Coordinating State Systems,* Edmund Gleazer, Roger Yarrington
7. *From Class to Mass Learning,* William Birenbaum
8. *Humanizing Student Services,* Clyde Blocker
1975—9. *Using Instructional Technology,* George Voegel
10. *Reforming College Governance,* Richard Richardson

NEW DIRECTIONS FOR INSTITUTIONAL RESEARCH
Sidney Suslow, Editor-in-Chief
Paul Jedamus, Associate Editor

1974—1. *Evaluating Institutions for Accountability*, Howard Bowen
2. *Assessing Faculty Effort*, James Doi
3. *Toward Affirmative Action*, Lucy Sells
4. *Organizing Nontraditional Study*, Samuel Baskin
1975—5. *Evaluating Statewide Boards*, Robert Berdahl
6. *Assuring Academic Progress Without Growth*, Allan Cartter